Macmillan McGraw-Hill

Math Connects

1

Volume 2

Authors

Altieri • Balka • Day • Gonsalves • Grace • Krulik
Malloy • Molix-Bailey • Moseley • Mowry • Myren
Price • Reynosa • Santa Cruz • Silbey • Vielhaber

Mc Graw Hill Macmillan/McGraw-Hill

About the Cover

Plane figures and solid figures are featured topics First grade. The triangle on the boat is an example of a plane figure. The shape of the lighthouse is an example of a solid figure. Ask students to identify other solid and plane figures on the cover.

The McGraw·Hill Companies

 Macmillan/McGraw-Hill

Send all inquiries to:
Macmillan/McGraw-Hill
8787 Orion Place
Columbus, OH 43240-4027

Volume 2
ISBN: 978-0-02-105726-9
MHID: 0-02-105726-5

Math Connects Grade 1

Printed in the United States of America.

14 15 16 17 18 19 20 WEB 23 22 21 20 19 18 17

Contents in Brief

Focal Points and Connections
See page iv for key.

The Curriculum Focal Points identify key mathematical ideas for this grade. They are not discrete topics or a checklist to be mastered; rather, they provide a framework for the majority of instruction at a particular grade level and the foundation for future mathematics study. The complete document may be viewed at www.nctm.org/focalpoints.

KEY

G1-FP1
Grade 1 Focal Point 1

G1-FP2
Grade 1 Focal Point 2

G1-FP3
Grade 1 Focal Point 3

G1-FP4C
Grade 1 Focal Point 4
Connection

G1-FP5C
Grade 1 Focal Point 5
Connection

G1-FP6C
Grade 1 Focal Point 6
Connection

G1-FP1 *Number and Operations* and *Algebra:* **Developing understandings of addition and subtraction and strategies for basic addition facts and related subtraction facts**

Children develop strategies for adding and subtracting whole numbers on the basis of their earlier work with small numbers. They use a variety of models, including discrete objects, length-based models (e.g., lengths of connecting cubes), and number lines, to model "part-whole," "adding to," "taking away from," and "comparing" situations to develop an understanding of the meanings of addition and subtraction and strategies to solve such arithmetic problems. Children understand the connections between counting and the operations of addition and subtraction (e.g., adding two is the same as "counting on" two). They use properties of addition (commutativity and associativity) to add whole numbers, and they create and use increasingly sophisticated strategies based on these properties (e.g., "making tens") to solve addition and subtraction problems involving basic facts. By comparing a variety of solution strategies, children relate addition and subtraction as inverse operations.

G1-FP2 *Number and Operations:* **Developing an understanding of whole number relationships, including grouping in tens and ones**

Children compare and order whole numbers (at least to 100) to develop an understanding of and solve problems involving the relative sizes of these numbers. They think of whole numbers between 10 and 100 in terms of groups of tens and ones (especially recognizing the numbers 11 to 19 as 1 group of ten and particular numbers of ones). They understand the sequential order of the counting numbers and their relative magnitudes and represent numbers on a number line.

G1-FP3 *Geometry:* **Composing and decomposing geometric shapes**

Children compose and decompose plane and solid figures (e.g., by putting two congruent isosceles triangles together to make a rhombus), thus building an understanding of part-whole relationships as well as the properties of the original and composite shapes. As they combine figures, they recognize them from different perspectives and orientations, describe their geometric attributes and properties, and determine how they are alike and different, in the process developing a background for measurement and initial understandings of such properties as congruence and symmetry.

G1-FP4C *Number and Operations* and *Algebra:* Children use mathematical reasoning, including ideas such as commutativity and associativity and beginning ideas of tens and ones, to solve two-digit addition and subtraction problems with strategies that they understand and can explain. They solve both routine and nonroutine problems.

G1-FP5C **Measurement and *Data Analysis:*** Children strengthen their sense of number by solving problems involving measurements and data. Measuring by laying multiple copies of a unit end to end and then counting the units by using groups of tens and ones supports children's understanding of number lines and number relationships. Representing measurements and discrete data in picture and bar graphs involves counting and comparisons that provide another meaningful connection to number relationships.

G1-FP6C *Algebra:* Through identifying, describing, and applying number patterns and properties in developing strategies for basic facts, children learn about other properties of numbers and operations, such as odd and even (e.g., "Even numbers of objects can be paired, with none left over"), and 0 as the identity element for addition.

Reprinted with permission from *Curriculum Focal Points for Prekindergarten through Grade 8 Mathematics: A Quest for Coherence,* copyright 2006 by the National Council of Teachers of Mathematics. All rights reserved.

v

Authors

Mary Behr Altieri
Putnam/Northern
Westchester BOCES
Yorktown Heights,
New York

Don S. Balka
Professor Emeritus
Saint Mary's College
Notre Dame, Indiana

Roger Day, Ph.D.
Mathematics Department Chair
Pontiac Township High School
Pontiac, Illinois

Philip D. Gonsalves
Mathematics Coordinator
Alameda County Office
of Education and
California State
University East Bay
Hayward, California

Ellen C. Grace
Consultant
Albuquerque,
New Mexico

Stephen Krulik
Professor Emeritus
Mathematics Education
Temple University
Cherry Hill, New Jersey

Carol E. Malloy, Ph.D.
Associate Professor of
Mathematics Education
University of North
Carolina at Chapel Hill
Chapel Hill, North
Carolina

Rhonda J. Molix-Bailey
Mathematics Consultant
Mathematics by Design
Desoto, Texas

Lois Gordon Moseley
Staff Developer
NUMBERS: Mathematics
Professional
Development
Houston, Texas

Brian Mowry
Independent Math Educational
Consultant/Part-Time Pre-K
Instructional Specialist
Austin Independent School District
Austin, Texas

Math Online Meet the Authors at macmillanmh.com

Christina L. Myren
Consultant Teacher
Conejo Valley Unified
    School District
Thousand Oaks, California

Jack Price
Professor Emeritus
California State
    Polytechnic University
Pomona, California

Mary Esther Reynosa
Instructional Specialist for
    Elementary Mathematics
Northside Independent
    School District
San Antonio, Texas

Rafaela M. Santa Cruz
SDSU/CGU Doctoral
    Program in Education
San Diego State University
San Diego, California

Robyn Silbey
Math Content Coach
Montgomery County
    Public Schools
Gaithersburg, Maryland

Kathleen Vielhaber
Mathematics Consultant
St. Louis, Missouri

Contributing Authors

Donna J. Long
Mathematics Consultant
Indianapolis, Indiana

FOLDABLES Dinah Zike
Educational Consultant
Dinah-Might Activities, Inc.
San Antonio, Texas

Consultants

Macmillan/McGraw-Hill wishes to thank the following professionals for their feedback. They were instrumental in providing valuable input toward the development of this program in these specific areas.

Mathematical Content

Viken Hovsepian
Professor of Mathematics
Rio Hondo College
Whittier, California

Grant A. Fraser, Ph.D.
Professor of Mathematics
California State University, Los Angeles
Los Angeles, California

Arthur K. Wayman, Ph.D.
Professor of Mathematics Emeritus
California State University, Long Beach
Long Beach, California

Assessment

Jane D. Gawronski, Ph.D.
Director of Assessment and Outreach
San Diego State University
San Diego, California

Cognitive Guided Instruction

Susan B. Empson, Ph.D.
Associate Professor of Mathematics
  and Science Education
University of Texas at Austin
Austin, Texas

English Learners

Cheryl Avalos
Mathematics Consultant
Los Angeles County Office of Education, Retired
Hacienda Heights, California

Kathryn Heinze
Graduate School of Education
Hamline University
St. Paul, Minnesota

Family Involvement

Paul Giganti, Jr.
Mathematics Education Consultant
Albany, California

Literature

David M. Schwartz
Children's Author, Speaker, Storyteller
Oakland, California

Vertical Alignment

Berchie Holliday
National Educational Consultant
Silver Spring, Maryland

Deborah A. Hutchens, Ed.D.
Principal
Norfolk Highlands Elementary
Chesapeake, Virginia

Reviewers

Each Reviewer reviewed at least two chapters of the Student Edition, giving feedback and suggestions for improving the effectiveness of the mathematics instruction.

Ernestine D. Austin
Facilitating Teacher/
    Basic Skills Teacher
LORE School
Ewing, NJ

Susie Bellah
Kindergarten Teacher
Lakeland Elementary
Humble, Texas

Megan Bennett
Elementary Math Coordinator
Hartford Public Schools
Hartford, CT

Susan T. Blankenship
5th Grade Teacher – Math
Stanford Elementary School
Stanford, KY

Wendy Buchanan
3rd Grade Teacher
The Classical Center at Vial
Garland, Texas 75043

Sandra Signorelli Coelho
Associate Director for
    Mathematics
PIMMS at Wesleyan University
Middletown, CT

Joanne DeMizio
Asst. Supt., Math and Science
    Curriculum
Archdiocese of New York
New York, NY

Anthony Dentino
Supervisor of Mathematics
Brick Township Schools
Brick, NJ

Lorrie L. Drennon
Math Teacher
Collins Middle School
Corsicana, TX 75110

Ethel A. Edwards
Director of Curriculum and
    Instruction
Topeka Public Schools
Topeka, Kansas

Carolyn Elender
District Elementary Math
    Instructional Specialist
Pasadena ISD
Pasadena, Texas

Monica Engel
Educator Second Grade
Pioneer Elementary School
Bolingbrook, IL

Anna Dahinden Flynn
Math Teacher
Coulson Tough K–6 Elementary
The Woodlands, TX

Brenda M. Foxx
Principal
University Park Elementary
University Park, MD

Katherine A. Frontier
Elementary Teacher
Laidlaw
Western Springs, IL

Susan J. Furphy
5th Grade Teacher
Nisley Elementary
Grand Jct., CO 81503

Peter Gatz
Student Services Coordinator
Brooks Elementary
Aurora, IL

Amber Gregersen
Teacher – 2nd Grade
Nisley Elementary
Grand Junction, Colorado

Roberta Grindle
Math and Language Arts
    Academic Intervention
    Service Provider
Cumberland Head Elementary
    School
Plattsburgh, NY

Sr. Helen Lucille Habig, RSM
Assistant Superintendent/
    Mathematics
Archdiocese of Cincinnati
Cincinnati, Ohio

Holly L. Hepp
Math Facilitator
Barringer Academic Center
Charlotte, NC

Martha J. Hickman
2nd Grade Teacher
Dr. James Craik Elementary
    School
Pomfret, MD

Margie Hill
District Coordinating Teacher for
    Mathematics, K–12
Blue Valley USD 229
Overland Park, Kansas

Carol H. Joyce
5th Grade Teacher
Nathanael Greene Elementary
Liberty, NC

Stella K. Kostante
Curriculum Coach
Roosevelt Elementary
Pittsburgh, PA

Pamela Fleming Lowe
Fourth Grade eMINTS Teacher
O'Neal Elementary
Poplar Bluff, Missouri

Lauren May, NBCT
4th Grade Teacher
May Watts Elementary School
Naperville, IL

Lorraine Moore
Grade 3 Math Teacher
Cowpens Elementary School
Cowpens, SC

Shannon L. Moorhead
4th Grade Teacher
Centerville Elementary
Anderson, SC

Gina M. Musselman, M.Ed
Kindergarten Teacher
Padeo Verde Elementary
Peoria, AZ

Jen Neufeld
3rd Grade Teacher
Kendall
Naperville, IL

Cathie Osiecki
K-5 Mathematics Coordinator
Middletown Public Schools
Middletown, CT

Phyllis L. Pacilli
Elementary Education Teacher
Fullerton Elementary
Addison, IL

Cindy Pearson
4th/5th Grade Teacher
John D. Spicer Elementary
Haltom City, TX 76137

Herminio M. Planas
Mathematics Curriculum
    Specialist
Administrative Offices-Bridgeport
    Public Schools
Bridgeport, Connecticut

Jo J. Puree
Educator
Lackamas Elementary
Yelm, WA

Teresa M. Reynolds
Third Grade Teacher
Forrest View Elementary
Everett, WA

Dr. John A. Rhodes
Director of Mathematics
Indian Prairie SD #204
Aurora, IL

Amy Romm
1st Grade Teacher
Starline Elementary
Lake Havasu, AZ

Delores M. Rushing
Numeracy Coach
Dept. of Academic Services-
    Mathematics Department
Washington, DC

Daniel L. Scudder
Mathematics/Technology
    Specialist
Boone Elementary
Houston, Texas

Laura Seymour
Resource Teacher Leader –
    Elementary Math & Science,
    Retired
Dearborn Public Schools
Dearborn, MI

Petra Siprian
Teacher
Army Trail Elementary School
Addison, IL

Sandra Stein
K-5 Mathematics Consultant
St. Clair County Regional
    Educational Service Agency
Marysville, MI

Barb Stoflet
Curriculum Specialist
Roseville Area Schools
Roseville, MN

Kim Summers
Principal
Dynard Elementary
Chaptico, MD

Ann C. Teater
4th Grade Teacher
Lancaster Elementary
Lancaster, KY

Anne E. Tunney
Teacher
City of Erie School District
Erie, PA

Joylien Weathers
1st Grade Teacher
Mesa View Elementary
Grand Junction, CO 81503

Christine F. Weiss
Third Grade Teacher
Robert C. Hill Elementary School
Romeoville, IL

Contents

Start Smart

Contents

= Hands-On Activity

Focal Points and Connections
See page iv for key.

G1-FP2 *Number and Operations*

H.O.T. Problems
Higher Order Thinking 36

Problem Solving 18, 28, 30, 40

WRITING IN ▸MATH 20

xi

Contents

Focal Points and Connections
See page iv for key.

G1-FP1 *Number and Operations* and *Algebra*

H.O.T. Problems
Higher Order Thinking 54, 60, 66, 76

Problem Solving 52, 68

WRITING IN MATH 56

Contents

 = Hands-On Activity

 = Technology Link

Focal Points and Connections
See page iv for key.

G1-FP1 *Number and Operations* and *Algebra*

H.O.T. Problems
Higher Order Thinking 92, 102, 104

Problem Solving 88, 96, 112

WRITING IN ▶MATH 90

Contents

Focal Points and Connections
See page iv for key.

G1-FP5C *Measurement* and *Data Analysis*

H.O.T. Problems
Higher Order Thinking 140, 144

Problem Solving 124, 126

WRITING IN ▶ MATH 130

xiv

CHAPTER 5

Develop Addition Strategies

= Hands-On Activity

Focal Points and Connections
See page iv for key.

G1-FP2 *Number and Operations*
G1-FP6C *Algebra*

H.O.T. Problems
Higher Order Thinking 156, 170

Problem Solving 166, 172

WRITING IN ▶MATH 158

Contents

Focal Points and Connections
See page iv for key.

G1-FP2 *Number* and *Operations*
G1-FP6C *Algebra*

H.O.T. Problems
Higher Order Thinking 200

Problem Solving 186, 198

Writing in ►Math 196

Contents

 = Hands-On Activity

Focal Points and Connections
See page iv for key.

G1-FP5C *Measurement* and *Data Analysis*

H.O.T. Problems
Higher Order Thinking 226

Problem Solving 214, 216

WRITING IN ▶MATH 218

Contents

Focal Points and Connections
See page iv for key.

G1-FP2 *Number and Operations*

H.O.T. Problems
Higher Order Thinking 244, 260

Problem Solving 246, 256, 264

Writing in ►MATH 252

Contents

 = Hands-On Activity

 = Technology Link

Focal Points and Connections
See page iv for key.

G1-FP2 *Number and Operations*
G1-FP5C *Measurement* and *Data Analysis*

H.O.T. Problems
Higher Order Thinking 304

Problem Solving 280, 294, 298, 306

WRITING IN MATH 278

Contents

Focal Points and Connections
See page iv for key.

G1-FP2 *Number and Operations*
G1-FP6C *Algebra*

H.O.T. Problems
Higher Order Thinking 320, 324, 332

Problem Solving 318, 330

Writing in ►MATH 338

SEAL ISLAND

XX

Contents

 = Hands-On Activity

 = Technology Link

Focal Points and Connections
See page iv for key.

G1-FP4C *Number and Operations* and *Algebra*

H.O.T. Problems
Higher Order Thinking 354

Problem Solving 352, 356, 358, 372

WRITING IN ►MATH 364

xxi

Contents

Focal Points and Connections
See page iv for key.

G1-FP3 *Geometry*

H.O.T. Problems
Higher Order Thinking 396, 406

Problem Solving 388, 392, 404

Writing in ►MATH 386

CHAPTER 13

Understand Place Value

= Hands-On Activity

Tech Link = Technology Link

Focal Points and Connections
See page iv for key.

G1-FP2 *Number and Operations*

H.O.T. Problems
Higher Order Thinking 422

Problem Solving 436, 440, 444, 446

WRITING IN ►MATH 424

Contents

Focal Points and Connections
See page iv for key.

G1-FP3 *Geometry*

H.O.T. Problems
Higher Order Thinking 464

Problem Solving 458, 462

WRITING IN MATH 470

xxiv

CHAPTER
15

Solve Two-Digit Addition and Subtraction Problems

 = Hands-On Activity

Focal Points and Connections
See page iv for key.

G1-FP4C *Number and Operations* and *Algebra*

H.O.T. Problems
Higher Order Thinking 488

Problem Solving 492, 496, 500, 502

WRITING IN ►MATH 506

Contents

Looking Ahead

H.O.T. Problems
Higher Order Thinking LA10

Problem Solving LA4, LA6, LA12, LA14

WRITING IN ►MATH LA8

Contents

Problem-Solving Projects

Contents

Student Handbook

Compare Measurements

Key Vocabulary

length
measure
unit
weight

Explore

Put an X on the tallest.
Circle the shortest.

Name _____

 Are You Ready for Chapter 9?

Circle the longer one.

1.

2.

Underline the object that is heavier.

3.

4.

Put an **X** on the container that holds less.

5.

6.

Look at the string.

7. _____

Find something that is longer. _____

Find something that is shorter. _____

This page checks skills needed for Chapter 9.

MATH at HOME

Dear Family,

Today my class started Chapter 9, **Compare Measurements**. In this chapter, I will learn about length, weight, capacity, temperature, and area. Here is an activity we can do and a list of books we can read together.

Love,

_____

Activity

Tape pages of newsprint together to make a long strip. On the strip trace the outline of your hand with fingers spread and use different objects, such as books or shoes, to measure the length of the outline. Repeat and trace your child's hand. Compare the measurements.

Key Vocabulary

measure to find the length, height, or weight using standard or nonstandard units

Math Online ▷ Click on the eGlossary link at macmillanmh.com to find out more about these words. There are 13 languages.

Books to Read

Who Sank the Boat?
by Pamela Allen
Putnam Juvenile, 1996.

A Pig is Big
by Douglas Florian
Greenwillow Books, 2000.

Biggest, Strongest, Fastest
by Steve Jenkins
Houghton Mifflin Company, 1997.

MATEMÁTICAS en CASA

Estimada familia:

Hoy mi clase comenzó el Capítulo 9, **Compara medidas**. En este capítulo, aprenderé sobre la longitud, el peso y el volumen. A continuación, hay una actividad que podemos hacer y una lista de libros que podemos leer juntos.

Cariños,

_____

Actividad

Unan varias páginas de periódico con cinta adhesiva para hacer una tira larga. Dibujen el contorno de su hijo(a) sobre el papel y usen diferentes objetos, como libros o zapatos, para medir la longitud del contorno. Repitan el ejercicio y dibujen sus siluetas. Comparen las medidas.

Vocabulario clave

medir calcular la longitud, el peso o el volumen en base a comparaciones

Math Online Visiten el enlace eGlossary en macmillanmh.com para averiguar más sobre estas palabras, las cuales se muestran en 13 idiomas.

Libros recomendados

¿Hay algo más grande que una ballena azul?
de Robert E. Wells
Editorial Juventud, 2000.

Carrie está a la altura
de Linda Williams Aber
The Kane Press, 2005.

Dime que tan lejos esta de aqui (los estupendos whiz kids)
de Shirley Willis
Franklin Watts, 2000.

Name _____

Compare and Order Lengths

Get Ready

Main Idea

I will compare and order the length of objects.

Vocabulary

length

short / shorter / shortest

long / longer / longest

You can compare the length of objects.

The eraser is shortest.

The book is longer than the pencil.

Check

Find the objects in your classroom. Compare.
Circle the object.

1. Which is shorter?

2. Which is longer?

3. Order the lengths from shortest to longest.
Write 1, 2, or 3.

_____   _____   _____

4. **Talk About It** What else could you use to compare lengths?

Find the objects in your classroom. Compare.
Circle the object.

5. Which is shorter?

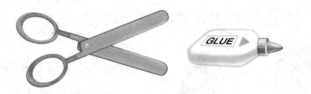

6. Which is longer?

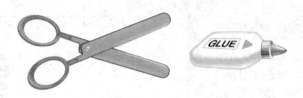

---

7. Order the lengths from longest to shortest.
Write 1, 2, or 3.

____   ____   ____

---

8. Order the lengths from shortest to longest.
Write 1, 2, or 3.

____   ____   ____

---

9. WRITING IN ►MATH How would Exercise 8 change
if you ordered the lengths from longest to shortest?

_____

_ _

_ _

Math at Home Activity: Find two objects in the kitchen and have your
child describe them by comparing their lengths.

Name _____

Nonstandard Units of Length

Get Ready

Main Idea

I will measure using nonstandard units.

Vocabulary

measure

unit

You can **measure** to find length.
A cube or a paper clip is one **unit**.

I can use cubes to measure.

I can use paper clips to measure.

Check

Remember
Line up the end of the pencil exactly with the end of the cube.

Use  to measure.

1. about ___8___

2. about _____

3. about _____

4. **Talk About It** How can you tell which pencil on this page is the longest?

(tcl cl)Dorling Kindersley, (tc)Richard Hutchings, (bcl)Emma Lee/Getty Images

Use to measure.

We can measure with cubes.

5.

about _____

6.

about _____

7.

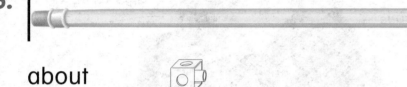

about _____

Problem Solving

8. Visual Thinking

Draw a pencil that is shorter.

Draw a pencil that is longer.

Math at Home Activity: Have your child use a nonstandard unit (such as a paper clip or macaroni) to measure and compare objects.

Name _____

Problem-Solving Strategy
Guess and Check

Main Idea

I will guess and check to solve a problem.

How many cubes long is the carrot?

Understand

What do I need to find?
Circle the question.

Plan

How will I solve the problem?

Solve

Guess and Check

_____ cubes

Check

Look back.
Is my answer reasonable?

Try It

About how many  long is each object?
Guess. Then measure.

Remember
Understand
Plan
Solve
Check

1.

Guess: about _____ cubes

Measure: about _____ cubes

2.

Guess: about _____ cubes

Measure: about _____ cubes

3.

Guess: about _____ cubes

Measure: about _____ cubes

4.

Guess: about _____ cubes

Measure: about _____ cubes

282 two hundred eighty-two

 **Math at Home Activity:** Ask your child to guess how many paper clips long his or her shoe is. Then, check it using actual paper clips.

Name _____

Find the object.	Circle the unit.	Measure the object.
1.		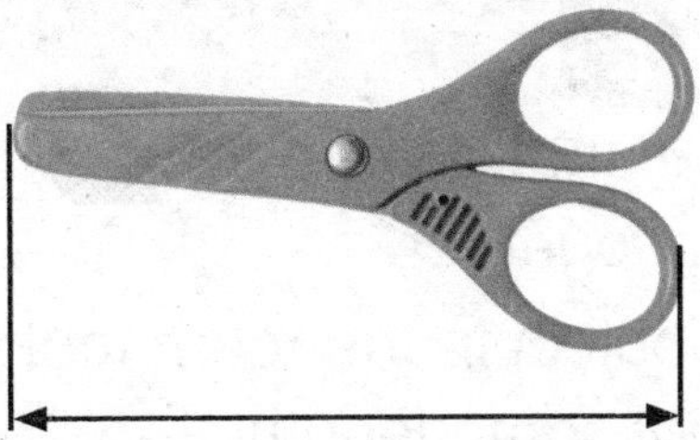 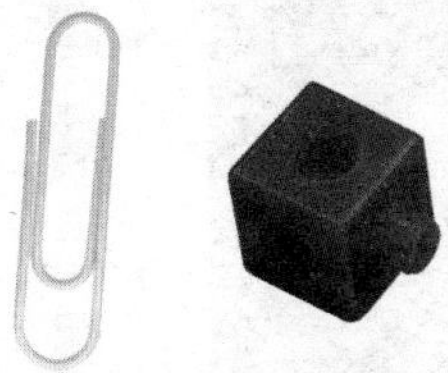 about ____
2.		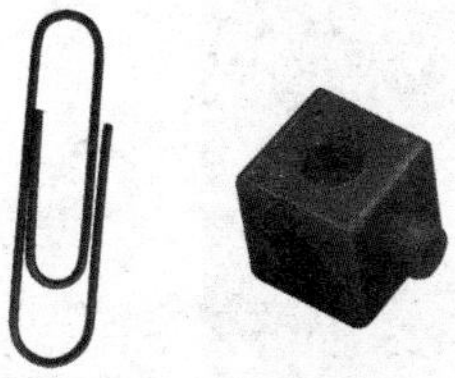 about ____
3.		 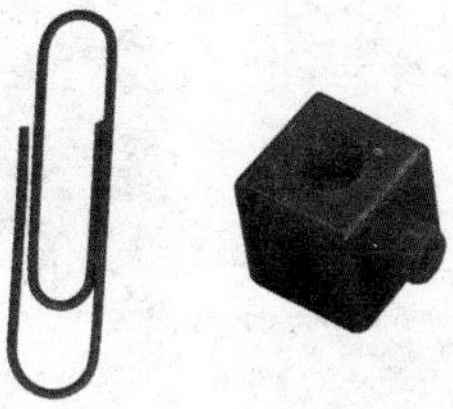 about ____
4.		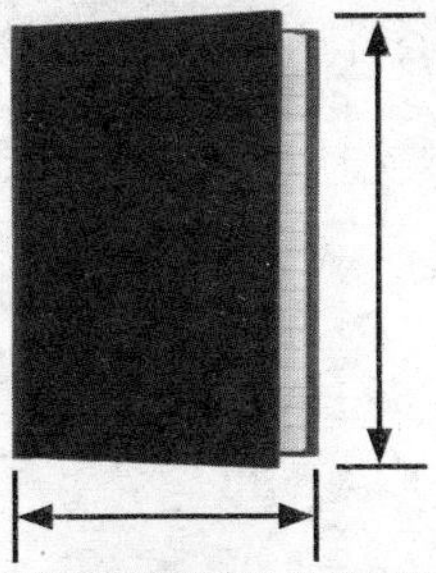 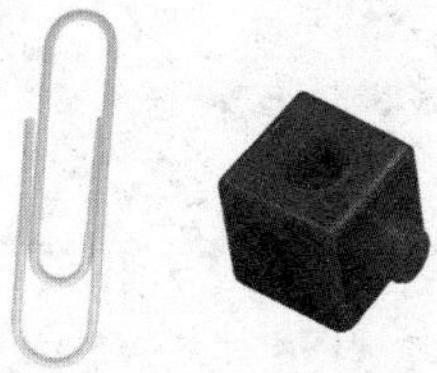 about ____ about ____
5.		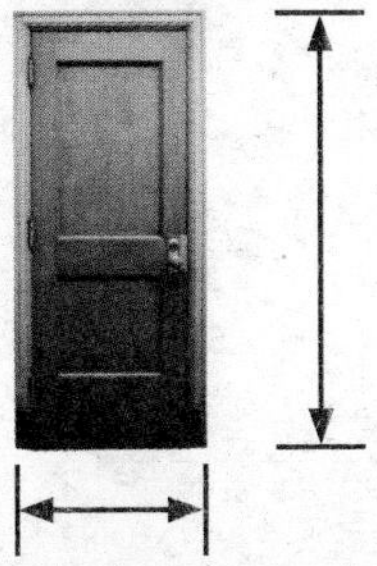 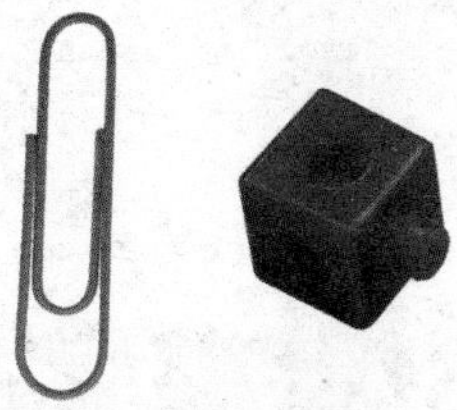 about ____ about ____
6.		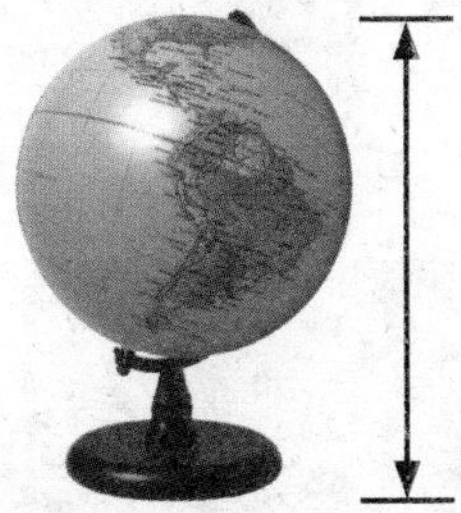 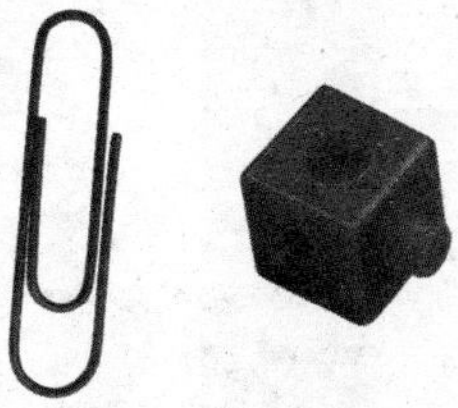 about ____

Game Time

Busy Beavers
Length

What You Need

Play with a partner. Take turns.
- Roll the 🎲.
- Count out that number of 🔲 and put them together.
- Find an object in the room that is about that same length.
- Do not repeat objects.
- Move your ♟ one space if you find an object.
- The first person to Finish wins!

Start

finish

Name _____

Compare and Order Weights

Main Idea

I will compare and order the weight of objects.

Vocabulary

weight

heavy/heavier/ heaviest

light/lighter/ lightest

You can compare the weights of objects. Some are **heavy** and some are **light**.

lighter

heavier

Check

Find the objects in your classroom. Compare.
Circle the object.

1. Which is heavier?

2. Which is lighter?

3. Order the objects by weight.
Write 1 for light, 2 for lighter, and 3 for lightest.

_____   _____   _____

(tcr)Richard Hutchings, (cl)The McGraw-Hill Companies/Stephen Ogilvy, (cr)Dorling Kindersley, (bc)Michael Newman/PhotoEdit, (bcr)Getty Images, (br)PhotoLink/Getty Images

Find the objects in your classroom. Compare.
Circle the object.

4. Which is heavier?

5. Which is lighter?

6. Which is heaviest?

7. Which is lighter?

Order the objects by weight.
Write 1 for heavy, 2 for heavier, and 3 for heaviest.

8.

_____   _____   _____

Write 1 for light, 2 for lighter, and 3 for lightest.

9.

_____   _____   _____

10. **Talk About It** Describe two objects that weigh the same.

GO on

Name _____

Find the objects in your classroom. Compare.
Circle the object.

11. Which is lighter?

12. Which is heavier?

13. Which is lightest?

14. Which is heaviest?

Order the objects by weight.
Write 1 for heavy, 2 for heavier, and 3 for heaviest.

15.

_____ _____ _____

Order objects by weight.
Write 1 for light, 2 for lighter, and 3 for lightest.

16.

_____ _____ _____

17.

  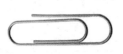

_____ _____ _____

Data File

Geckos are a type of lizard found in Arizona.

18. Put these geckos in order by length.

Write 1 for longest, 2, and 3 for shortest.

_____ _____ _____

Math at Home Activity Have your child compare two or three objects using the words heavier/heaviest and lighter/lightest.

Name _____

Compare. Circle the objects.

1. Which is shorter?

2. Which is longer?

3. Order the lengths from shortest to longest. Write 1, 2, and 3.

_____   _____   _____

Compare. Circle the objects.

4. Which is heavier?

5. Which is lighter?

6.

Tim used  to measure.

Then he used to measure.

Did he use more  or ☐ ? _____

Make two patterns. Use ▰ and ■. Draw your patterns.

7.

8.

Find each sum.

9. 5 + 2 = _____   **10.** 2 + 3 = _____   **11.** 8 + 1 = _____

12. 4 + 0 = _____   **13.** 3 + 3 = _____   **14.** 6 + 3 = _____

Find each difference.

15. 6 − 2 = _____   **16.** 5 − 3 = _____   **17.** 8 − 7 = _____

18. 5 − 4 = _____   **19.** 3 − 1 = _____   **20.** 7 − 6 = _____

Draw the missing hands to show each time.

21. half past 7   **22.** 1 o'clock   **23.** 30 minutes after 7

| : |

| : |

| : |

Formative Assessment

Name _____

Compare and Order Capacities

Main Idea

I will compare and order the capacity of objects.

Vocabulary

holds more/ most

holds less/ least

Containers can hold different amounts.

The glass holds less than the pitcher. The pitcher holds more than the glass. Capacity tells how much something holds.

Check

Circle the object in each pair that holds less.

1.

2.

Circle the object in each pair that holds more.

3.

4.

Circle the object that holds the least.

5.

6.

Order the objects by capacity.
Write 1 for holds the least, 2, and 3 for holds the most.

7.

_____ _____ _____

8.

_____ _____ _____

9. **Talk About It** If you had 2 containers, how could you find out which container holds more?

GO on

Name _____

Circle the object in each pair that holds less.

10.

11.

12.

13.

Circle the object in each pair that holds more.

14.

15.

16.

17.

Circle the object that holds the least.

18.

(tc) Richard Hutchings, (cl) Alamy Images, (cl) © Ian O'Leary/Dorling Kindersley, (cr) Creatas Images/Jupiter Images, (bl) Getty Images, (br) Jules Frazier/Getty Images

Circle the object that holds the most.

19.

Order the objects by capacity.
Write 1 for holds the least, 2, and 3 for holds the most.

20.

_____ _____ _____

21.

_____ _____ _____

Problem Solving

22. Visual Thinking How many cubes in each?
Use cubes to help.

 _____ cubes _____ cubes

 Math at Home Activity: Give your child two containers that can hold liquid. Ask your child which container holds more. Test to see if your child is right.

Compare and Order Temperatures

Get Ready

Main Idea

I will compare and order objects by their temperature.

Vocabulary

hot/hotter/
hottest

cold/colder/
coldest

You can tell if objects are hot or cold.

This object is **hot**.   This object is **cold**.

You can order objects by how hot they are.

hot   **hotter**   **hottest**

You can order objects by how cold they are.

cold   **colder**   **coldest**

Circle *hot* or *cold* to describe the temperature.

1.

hot   cold

2.

hot   cold

Compare the objects. Circle the hottest.
Put an X on the coldest. Underline the object that is in between.

3.

Order the objects by temperature.
Write 1 for hot, 2 for hotter, and 3 for hottest.

4.

_____   _____   _____

Write 1 for cold, 2 for colder, and 3 for coldest.

5.

_____   _____   _____

6. What are more ways you can order objects by temperature?

GO on

Name _____

Circle *hot* or *cold* to describe the temperature.

7.

hot   cold

8.

hot   cold

9.

hot   cold

10.

hot   cold

Compare the objects. Circle the hottest.
Put an X on the coldest.
Underline the object that is in between.

11.

12.

Order the objects by temperature.
Write 1 for hot, 2 for hotter, and 3 for hottest.

13.

_____   _____   _____

Write 1 for cold, 2 for colder, and 3 for coldest.

14.

_____   _____   _____

Problem Solving

15. Reasoning Order the pictures by temperature.
Write 1 for cool, 2 for cold, 3 for warm, and 4 for hot.

_____   _____   _____   _____

Math at Home Activity: Show your child three or more objects. Ask your child to put the objects in order according to their temperature.

Name _____

Problem-Solving
Investigation

Our desks are each 4 staplers wide.
Steven and I put our desks together.
Then we had a big desk that was 8 staplers
wide. Tyra put her desk with ours.
How wide are all 3 desks?

Main Idea

I will choose
a strategy
to solve a
problem.

Your Mission:
Find the width of
the desks.

Understand

What do I know? Underline what you know.
What do I need to find? Circle it.

Plan

How will I solve the problem?

Solve

One way is to make a table.

3 desks are _____ staplers wide.

Check

Look back.
Is my answer reasonable?

Choose a strategy. Solve.

1. Leslie's pitcher held 5 glasses of juice. Tory and Shuka's pitchers each held the same amount as Leslie's pitcher. If all the juice was put together, how much would there be?

_____ glasses

2. Felix is lining up his toy cars. 10 cars are as long as one leg. How many cars are as long as 4 legs?

_____ cars

3. Taylor, Rona, and Julie measure their pets' lengths. Taylor's rabbit is 6 cubes long. Rona's cat is 11 cubes long. Julie's hamster is 3 cubes long. Who has the longest pet?

_____

Math at Home Activity: Take advantage of problem-solving opportunities during daily routines such as riding in the car, bedtime, doing laundry, putting away groceries, planning schedules, and so on.

Name _____

Compare Areas

Get Ready

Main Idea

I will compare the area of different shapes.

Vocabulary

cover more/
   most

cover less/
   least

Area is the space inside a shape.

covers more

covers less

Smaller shapes **cover less** area.

Larger shapes **cover more** area.

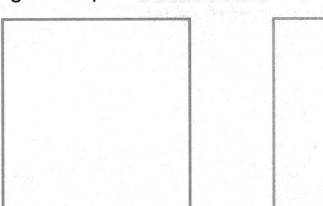

Use . Circle the shape that covers more area.

1.

2.

Use 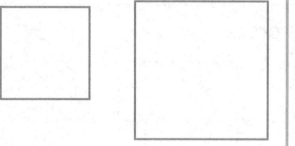. Mark an X on the shape that covers less area.

3.

4.

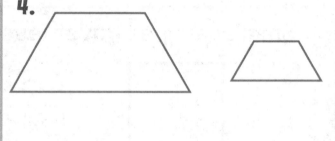

Use **blue** to color the shape that covers most.
Use red to color the shape that covers least.

5.

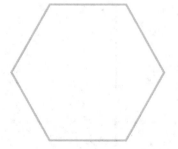

6. 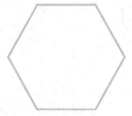 How can you tell which shape covers the most area?

Name _____

Use . Circle the shape that covers more area.

7.

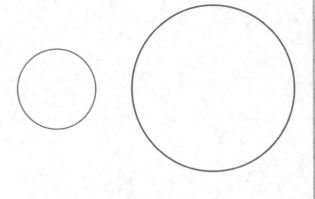

8.

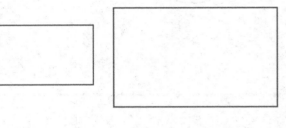

Use . Mark an X on the shape that covers less area.

9.

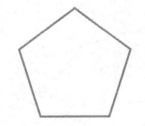

10.

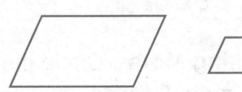

Use **blue** to color the shape that covers the most.
Use red to color the shape that covers the least.

11.

Use **blue** to color the shape that covers the most.
Use red to color the shape that covers the least.

12.

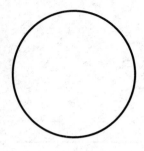 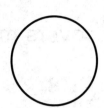

13.

 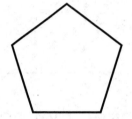

H.O.T. Problem

14. Thinking Math Circle the shape that covers the
most area. How do you know?

_____

_____

Math at Home Activity: Have your child compare books of different sizes.
Have them order the books from covers the most area to covers the least area.
Remind your child that larger shapes cover more area and smaller shapes cover
less area.

Name _____

Order Areas

Get Ready

Main Idea

I will order shapes by comparing how much area they cover.

Shapes can be ordered by area.

This shape covers the least area.

The shapes are ordered from covers the most area to covers the least area.

Check

Order the shapes by area. Write 1 for covers the most, 2 for covers less, and 3 for covers the least.

1.

____   ____   ____

Order the shapes by area. Write 1 for covers the least, 2 for covers more, and 3 for covers the most.

2.

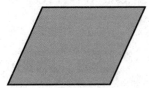

____   ____   ____

3. **Talk About It** What would happen if you put a large piece of paper on top of a small piece of paper?

Order the shapes by area. Write 1 for covers the most, 2 for covers less, and 3 for covers the least.

4.

 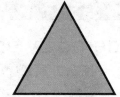

_____   _____   _____

5.

  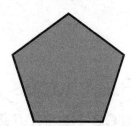

_____   _____   _____

Order the shapes by area. Write 1 for covers the least, 2 for covers more, and 3 for covers the most.

6.

_____   _____   _____

Problem Solving

7. Visual Thinking The triangle covers less area. The circle covers more area. Draw a shape that could go in the middle.

Math at Home Activity: Give your child a page of the newspaper, a piece of notebook paper and a post-it. Ask your child to order the area from covers most to covers least. To make the activity more challenging, cut the paper into various shapes.

The first graders at Gladmere Elementary collected juice boxes to recycle.

Monday Collection

Class	Juice Boxes Collected
Mrs. Wilson's Class	12
Ms. York's Class	8

How many juice boxes did the classes collect in all?

_____ boxes

FOLD DOWN

D

Problem Solving in Science

Real-World MATH

Finding new uses for things is called reusing. Using old items to make new things is recycling.

This book belongs to

_____

A

These tires have been
recycled for a playground!

C

These jars have been
reused as flower pots.

A

B

Which jar holds more? _____

B

Name _____

Vocabulary

Circle the word to finish the sentence.

1.

The chair is _____ than the scissors.

heavier   **lighter**

2.

The mug holds _____ than the glass.

more   **less**

Concepts

Circle the object in each pair that is lighter.

3.    **4.**

Circle the object in each pair that holds more.

5.     **6.**

(bl)Edward R. Degginger/Bruce Coleman Inc., (bcl)Dorling Kindersley/Getty Images, (bc)2006 Photos To Go, (bc)CORBIS, (bcr)Peter Fakler/Alamy Images

Circle the object in each pair that is hotter.

7.

8.

Write about how many .

9.

_____ cubes

10.

_____ cubes

11.

_____ cubes

12.

_____ cubes

Problem Solving

13. A piece of blue string is 8 paper clips long.
A piece of red string is 6 paper clips longer
than the blue string. How long is the red string?

_____ paper clips

Summative Assessment

Name _____

Listen as your teacher reads each problem.
Choose the correct answer.

1.

   1   2   5   7
  ◯   ◯   ◯   ◯

2.

   1   2   3   8
  ◯   ◯   ◯   ◯

3.

  ◯   ◯   ◯   ◯

4.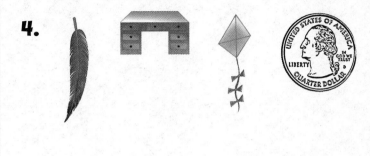

  ◯   ◯   ◯   ◯

5.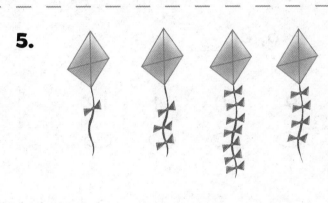

  ◯   ◯   ◯   ◯

6.

   18   46   62   70
  ◯   ◯   ◯   ◯

7.

⬭ ⬭ ⬭ ⬭

8. 4, 6, 8, _____

9   10   11   12

⬭   ⬭   ⬭   ⬭

9.

⬭   ⬭

⬭   ⬭

10.

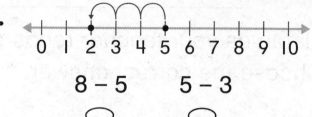

8 – 5   5 – 3

⬭   ⬭

10 – 8   7 – 3

⬭   ⬭

11. Tai saw 5 seals at the zoo. Jim saw 3 bears. How many animals did they see in all?

_____ animals

12. What number is 10 less than 75?

_____

STOP

Summative Assessment

CHAPTER 10

Solve Addition and Subtraction Problems

Review Vocabulary

doubles

doubles plus one

Explore

There were 7 birds on the cliff. 6 more landed. How many birds are there now?

_____ birds

Frans Lanting/Minden Pictures

Name _____

Are You Ready for Chapter 10?

Add or subtract.

1. $6 + 5 =$ _____   2. $7 - 3 =$ _____   3. $2 + 3 =$ _____

4. $\begin{array}{r} 9 \\ +\ 1 \\ \hline \end{array}$	5. $\begin{array}{r} 8 \\ +\ 4 \\ \hline \end{array}$	6. $\begin{array}{r} 3 \\ -\ 2 \\ \hline \end{array}$	7. $\begin{array}{r} 6 \\ -\ 3 \\ \hline \end{array}$

Use doubles to add or subtract.

8. $3 + 3 =$ _____   9. $12 - 6 =$ _____

10. $4 + 4 =$ _____   11. $10 - 5 =$ _____

12. $2 + 2 =$ _____   13. $8 - 4 =$ _____

14. $5 + 5 =$ _____   15. $6 - 3 =$ _____

16. There were 8 children at the party.
3 children left. How many
children are at the party now?

_____ children

This page checks skills needed for Chapter 10.

Dear Family,

Today my class started Chapter 10, **Solve Addition and Subtraction Problems**. In this chapter, I will learn to use strategies for addition and subtraction with numbers up to 20. Here is an activity we can do and a list of books we can read together.

Love,

_____

Activity

Take turns flipping through the pages of the phone book. Say "RRRRRING" to stop the flipping. Close your eyes and point to a number. Add the first two digits of the number together. Repeat using three numbers. Ask your child which two numbers they decided to add together first and why.

Review Vocabulary

doubles two addends that are the same number

$6 + 6 = 12$ $\qquad$ $9 + 9 = 18$

doubles plus one

$7 + 8 = 15$ $\qquad$ Think $7 + 7 = 14$

Math Online Click on the eGlossary link at macmillanmh.com to find out more about these words. There are 13 languages.

Books to Read

Twenty is Too Many
by Katie Duke
Dutton Juvenile, 2000.

Counting Wildflowers
by Bruce McMillan
HarperTrophy, 1995.

The Warlord's Beads
by Virginia Walton Pilegard
Pelican Publishing
Company, 2001.

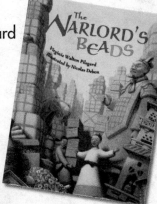

three hundred fifteen **315**

Estimada familia:

Hoy mi clase comenzó el Capítulo 10, **Resuelve problemas de suma y de resta.** En este capítulo, aprenderé a usar estrategias para sumar y restar con números hasta el 20. A continuación, hay una actividad que podemos hacer y una lista de libros que podemos leer juntos.

Cariños,

_____

Actividad

Túrnense en hojear las páginas de la guía telefónica. Digan "RRRRRING" para dejar de hojear. Cierren los ojos y señalen un número telefónico. Sumen los tres primeros dígitos del número. Pregúntenle a su hijo(a) qué par de números decidieron sumar primero y por qué.

Repaso de vocabulario

dobles operaciones donde los dos sumandos son iguales.

6 + 6 = 12   9 + 9 = 18

dobles más uno

7 + 8 = 15   Piensa 7 + 7 = 14

Math Online ⟩ Visiten el enlace eGlossary en macmillanmh.com para averiguar más sobre estas palabras, las cuales se muestran en 13 idiomas.

Libros recomendados

¿Cuantos osos hay?
de Cooper Edens
Antheneum Books, 1994.

Las semillas magicas
de Mitsumasa Anno
Fondo de cultura
Economica USA, 2005.

Name _____

Doubles

Main Idea

I will use doubles facts to add.

Review Vocabulary

doubles

The addends are the same in a doubles fact.

You can double the number to find the sum.

$6 + 6 = 12$

$8 + 8 = 16$

Check

Draw the missing dots to show a double.
Write the doubles fact.

Look at the sum to help you find the doubles fact.

1.

_____ + _____ = _____

2.

_____ + _____ = _____

Draw dots to show the doubles.
Write the addends.

3.

_____ + _____ = 10

4.

_____ + _____ = 8

5. **Talk About It** Can you use doubles to make 15?
Why or why not?

Draw the missing dots to show a double.
Write the doubles fact.

6.

_____ + _____ = _____

7.

_____ + _____ = _____

8.

_____ + _____ = _____

9.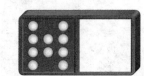

_____ + _____ = _____

Draw dots to show the doubles.
Write the addends.

10.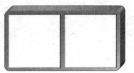

_____ + _____ = 18

11.

_____ + _____ = 8

12.

_____ + _____ = 12

13.

_____ + _____ = 6

Problem Solving

14. Critical Thinking How many doubles facts
can you make with your fingers? _____

Math at Home Activity: Say a number from 0-10. Have your child say
a doubles fact using that number.

Name _____

Doubles Plus 1

Main Idea

I will add doubles plus one.

Review Vocabulary

doubles plus 1

You can use doubles plus 1 to help you add.

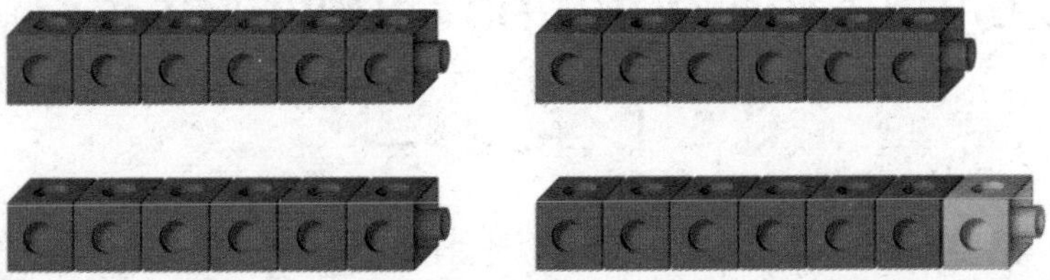

6 + 6 = 12
6 + 7 is one more so the pattern is to add one more.
6 + 7 = 13

Check

Use the pattern to find the sums.

1.

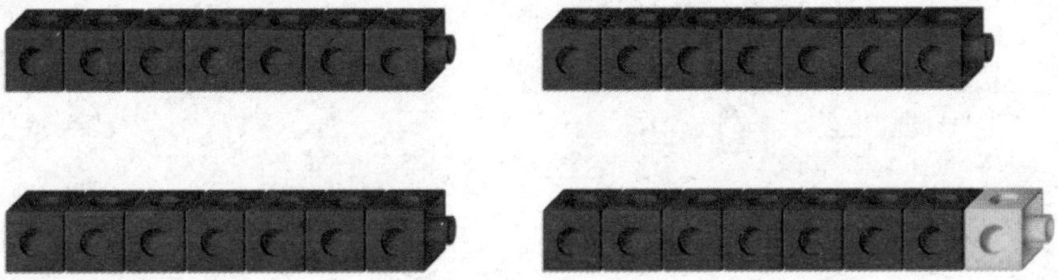

7 + 7 = __14__

7 + 8 = __15__

2.

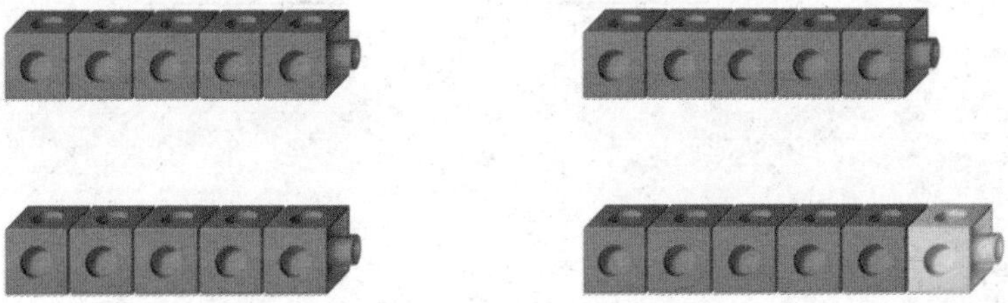

5 + 5 = ____

5 + 6 = ____

3. 4 + 4 = ____

4 + 5 = ____

4. 8 + 8 = ____

9 + 8 = ____

5. **Talk About It** How does knowing 4 + 4 help you find 4 + 5?

Practice

Use the pattern to find the sums.

    2 + 2 is a doubles fact.

6.

2 + 2 = ____

2 + 3 = ____

2 + 3 is a doubles plus one fact.

Find the sums. Circle the doubles plus 1 facts.

7. 1 + 1 = ____   1 + 2 = ____

8. 8 + 8 = ____   8 + 9 = ____

9. 7 + 7 = ____   7 + 8 = ____

10. 3 + 3 = ____   3 + 4 = ____

11. 9 + 9 = ____   9 + 10 = ____

12. 6   6   **13.**   8   8
       + 6   + 7   + 8   + 9
       ____   ____   ____   ____

H.O.T. Problem

14. Algebra What are the missing numbers?

8 + ____ = 15

____ + 7 = 11

9 + ____ = 18

Missing
4, 7, 9
Reward

Math at Home Activity: Hold up 8 fingers. Have your child name the doubles fact (8+8) and what the doubles plus 1 fact (8+9) would be.

Name _____

Find each sum. Use doubles to help you add.

1. 8 + 8 = _____   8 + 9 = _____   9 + 8 = _____

2.   7   7   8
   + 7   + 8   + 7
   _____   _____   _____

3.   5   4   4
   + 4   + 5   + 4
   _____   _____   _____

4.   5   6   5
   + 5   + 5   + 6
   _____   _____   _____

5.   9   8   9
   + 9   + 9   + 8
   _____   _____   _____

6.   7   6   6
   + 6   + 7   + 6
   _____   _____   _____

Now circle the doubles problem in each set.

Game Time

Circle Up
Adding Doubles

You Will Need

Play with a partner.
- Take turns rolling the ◻.
- Double the number you roll. If you are right, cover that number with a counter.
- If the number is already covered, take another turn.
- The player covering the most numbers wins.

Name _____

Make a 10 to Add

Get Ready

Main Idea

I will make a 10 to find sums.

You can make a 10 to help you add.

9 + 5 is equal to 9 + 1 + 4 which is equal to 10 + 4.

Check

Use WorkMat 1 and 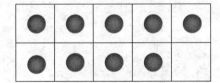 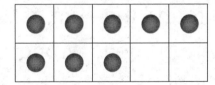. Draw the counters. Then add.

1.

9 + 4 = _____ , because

9 + 1 + 3 = _____ and

10 + 3 = _____

2.

8 + 5 = _____ , because

8 + 2 + 3 = _____ and

10 + 3 = _____

3.

9 + 2 = _____ , because

9 + 1 + _____ = _____ and

10 + _____ = _____

4.

8 + 4 = _____ , because

8 + 2 + _____ = _____ and

_____ + 2 = _____

5. **Talk About It** How does making a 10 help you find the sum?

Use WorkMat 1 and 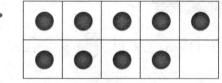 . Draw the counters. Then add.

6.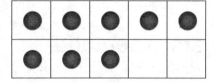

9 + 6 = _____, because

9 + 1 + 5 = _____ and

10 + 5 = _____

7.

8 + 7 = _____, because

8 + 2 + _____ = _____ and

_____ + 5 = _____

8.

8 + 6 = _____, because

8 + 2 + 4 = _____ and

10 + 4 = _____

9.

9 + 7 = _____, because

9 + _____ + 6 = _____ and

10 + _____ = _____

H.O.T. Problem

10. **Make It Right** This is how Jorge found the sum of 9 + 7. Tell why Jorge is wrong. Make it right.

_____

_ _ _ _ _ _ _ _ _ _ _ _ _

_____

_____

Math at Home Activity: Have your child use small objects to show how 7 + 4 and 10 + 1 are the same.

Name _____

Problem-Solving Strategy
Draw a Picture

Main Idea

I will draw a picture to solve a problem.

Alex saw 8 baby seals. Then he saw 6 more baby seals. How many baby seals did Alex see?

Understand

What do I know?
Underline what you know.
What do I need to find?
Circle the question.

Plan

How will I solve the problem?

Solve

Draw a picture.

_____ _____ ◯ _____ _____ ◯ _____ _____

_____ baby seals

Check

Look back.
Is my answer reasonable?

Try It

Draw a picture to solve.

1. Marissa saw 9 birds.
   She saw 4 fly away.
   How many were left?

_____ ◯ _____ = _____ birds

2. Ryan picked 5 apples.
   Maria picked 6 apples.
   How many apples did
   they pick in all?

_____ ◯ _____ = _____ apples

Your Turn

Draw a picture to solve.

3. There are 7 frogs in the pond.
   5 more frogs join them.
   How many frogs are in
   the pond now?

_____ ◯ _____ = _____ frogs

4. Amy planted 12 flowers in two rows.
   She planted 6 flowers in the first row.
   How many did she plant in the
   second row?

_____ ◯ _____ = _____ flowers

Math at Home Activity: Write a subtraction sentence for your child to solve. Encourage your child to draw a picture to help.

Name _____

Draw the missing dots to show a double.
Write the doubles fact.

1.

_____ + _____ = _____

2.

_____ + _____ = _____

Find the sums.

3. 4 + 4 = _____   4 + 5 = _____

4. 8 + 8 = _____   9 + 8 = _____

Draw the counters. Then add.

5.

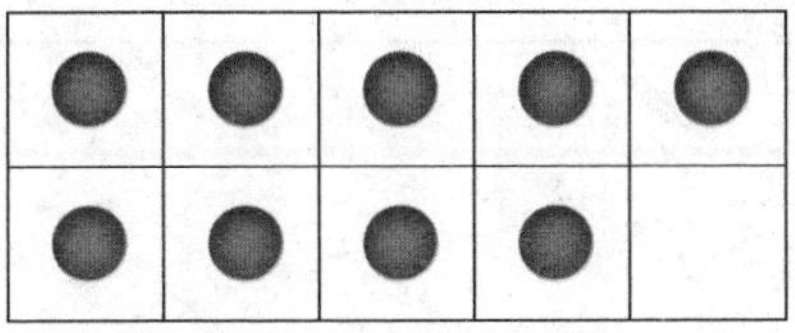

9 + 3 = _____

9 + 1 + _____ = _____

_____ + 2 = _____

6.

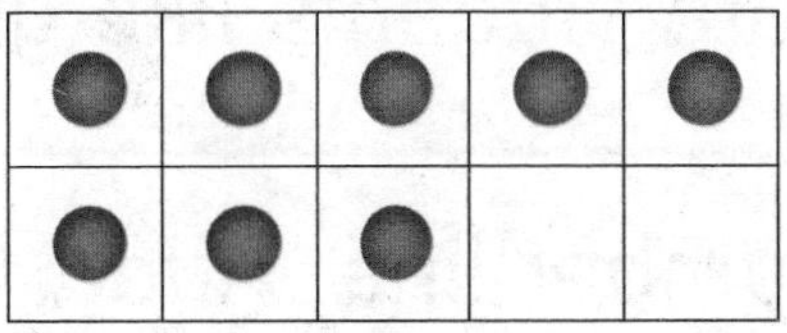

8 + 3 = _____

8 + _____ + _____ = _____

_____ + 1 = _____

7. Jada ate 8 grapes.
Lynn ate 6 more than Jada.
How many grapes did Lynn eat?

_____ ◯ _____ ◯ _____ grapes

Write each total. Then make the bar graph and answer the questions.

Favorite Color		
Subject	Tally	Total
Blue	﹩ HHT IIII	
Green	HHT	
Orange	HHT II	
Purple	II	

Favorite Color

	1	2	3	4	5	6	7	8	9	10
Blue										
Green										
Orange										
Purple										

8. Which color is liked most? _____

9. Which color is liked least? _____

10. Do more students like green or orange? _____

Use the number line. Add.

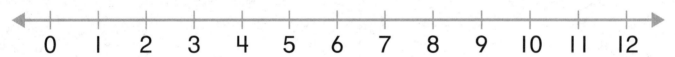

0 1 2 3 4 5 6 7 8 9 10 11 12

11. $2 + 7 =$ _____   12. $1 + 4 =$ _____   13. $9 + 3 =$ _____

Write the time.

14.

half past _____

15.

_____ : _____

16.

half past _____

Formative Assessment

Name _____

Use Doubles to Subtract

Get Ready

Main Idea

I will use doubles facts to subtract.

You can use addition facts to help you subtract.

I think 6 + 6 = 12
so 12 - 6 = 6.

6 + 6 = **12** 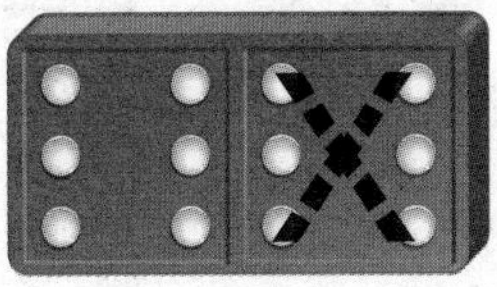   12 - 6 = **6**

Check

Add the doubles facts. Then subtract.

1. 2 + 2 = **4**
   4 - 2 = **2**

2. 3 + 3 = ____
   6 - 3 = ____

3.   5   10
    + 5   - 5

4.   1   2
    + 1   - 1

5.   9   18
    + 9   - 9

6.   7   14
    + 7   - 7

7. **Talk About It** How can using addition help you subtract?

Add the doubles facts. Then subtract.

8. 10 + 10 = _____

20 − 10 = _____

9. 4 + 4 = _____

8 − 4 = _____

10.
```
    8        16
  + 8       − 8
  ____      ____
```

11.
```
    6        12
  + 6       − 6
  ____      ____
```

Add or subtract.
Then draw a line to match the doubles fact.

12. 10 + 10 = _____

13. 9 + 9 = _____

14. 8 + 8 = _____

15. 7 + 7 = _____

14 − 7 = _____

16 − 8 = _____

18 − 9 = _____

20 − 10 = _____

Problem Solving

16. Number Sense A box has 12
crayons. You can only see 6.
How many crayons are hidden
in the box?

_____ ◯ _____ ◯ _____ crayons

Math at Home Activity: Give your child a doubles fact. Have them
give you a related subtraction fact.

Name _____

Relate Addition and Subtraction

Main Idea

I will use related addition and subtraction facts.

Find 16 − 7.

To find 16 − 7 I think ____ + 7 = 16.

9 + 7 = 16, so 16 − 7 = 9.

16 − 7 = __9__

✓ Check

Find each missing number.

1. 11 − 6 = __5__

   6 + __5__ = 11

2. 13 − 5 = ____

   5 + ____ = 13

3. 12 − 5 = ____

   5 + ____ = 12

4. 15 − 9 = ____

   9 + ____ = 15

Subtract. Write an addition fact that helps you subtract.

5. 10 − 6 = ____

   ____ + ____ = ____

6. 11 − 4 = ____

   ____ + ____ = ____

7. **Talk About It** 8 + 7 = 15. Tell the related subtraction facts. What pattern do you see?

Find each missing number.

8. 14 − 6 = _____

    6 + _____ = 14

9. 12 − 8 = _____

    8 + _____ = 12

10. 15 − 7 = _____

    7 + _____ = 15

11. 13 − 6 = _____

    6 + _____ = 13

12. 16 − 9 = _____

    9 + _____ = 16

13. 12 − 7 = _____

    7 + _____ = 12

14. 14 − 9 = _____

    9 + _____ = 14

15. 13 − 4 = _____

    4 + _____ = 13

Subtract. Write the addition fact that helps you subtract.

16. 14 − 5 = _____

    _____ + _____ = _____

17. 11 − 5 = _____

    _____ + _____ = _____

18. 13 − 8 = _____

    _____ + _____ = _____

19. 12 − 4 = _____

    _____ + _____ = _____

Problem Solving

20. **Number Sense** Write a word problem using the number sentences 4 + 7 = 11 or 11 − 4 = 7.

_____

_ _

Math at Home Activity: Have your child show related addition and subtraction facts using small objects.

Name _____

Problem-Solving Investigation

I have 18 students in my class.
Each student gets a flower.
I have 9.
How many more do I need?

Main Idea		Your Mission:
I will choose a strategy to solve a problem.		Find how many more flowers are needed.

Understand

What do I know? Underline what you know.

What do I need to find? Circle it.

Plan

How will I solve the problem?

Solve

One way is to write a number sentence.

_____ ◯ _____ = _____

_____ more flowers are needed.

Check

Look back.

Is my answer reasonable?

Choose a strategy. Solve.

1. Pablo has 5 leaves.
   Kaitlyn has 5 leaves.
   How many leaves do they
   have altogether?

_____ leaves

2. Martin found 7 shells.
   Pam found 8 shells.
   How many shells did they find in all?

_____ shells

3. Lina had 12 erasers.
   She gave her friends some of her erasers.
   Now she only has 6 erasers.
   How many erasers did she give away?

_____ erasers

4. 14 bees were outside the hive.
   Then 7 bees went inside the hive.
   How many bees were left outside?

_____ bees

Math at Home Activity: Take advantage of problem-solving opportunites during daily routines such as riding in the car, bedtime, doing laundry, putting away groceries, planning schedule, and so on.

Name _____

Fact Families

Copyright © Macmillan/McGraw-Hill, a division of The McGraw-Hill Companies, Inc.

Main Idea

I will make fact families.

Review Vocabulary

fact family

Facts that use the same numbers are called a fact family.

5, 9, and 14 are part of this fact family.

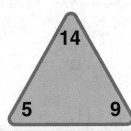

$5 + 9 = 14$ $14 - 5 = 9$

$9 + 5 = 14$ $14 - 9 = 5$

Check

Add or subtract. Complete each fact family.

1.

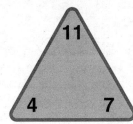

$7 + 4 = 11$ $11 - 7 = 4$

$4 + 7 = \underline{\hspace{1cm}}$ $11 - 4 = \underline{\hspace{1cm}}$

2.

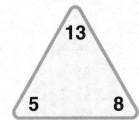

$5 + 8 = \underline{\hspace{1cm}}$ $13 - 5 = \underline{\hspace{1cm}}$

$8 + 5 = \underline{\hspace{1cm}}$ $13 - 8 = \underline{\hspace{1cm}}$

3.

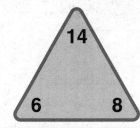

$6 + 8 = \underline{\hspace{1cm}}$ $14 - 6 = \underline{\hspace{1cm}}$

$8 + 6 = \underline{\hspace{1cm}}$ $14 - 8 = \underline{\hspace{1cm}}$

4. What fact family can you make with the numbers 8, 8, and 16?

Add or subtract. Complete each fact family.

5.

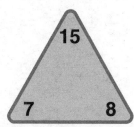

9 + 3 = _____   12 − 9 = _____

3 + 9 = _____   12 − 3 = _____

6.

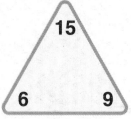

7 + 8 = _____   15 − 7 = _____

8 + 7 = _____   15 − 8 = _____

7.

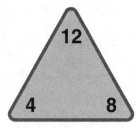

6 + 9 = _____   15 − 9 = _____

9 + 6 = _____   15 − 6 = _____

8.

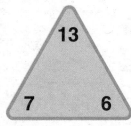

4 + 8 = _____   12 − 8 = _____

8 + 4 = _____   12 − 4 = _____

9.

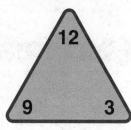

7 + 6 = _____   13 − 7 = _____

6 + 7 = _____   13 − 6 = _____

GO on

336   three hundred thirty-six

Math at Home Activity: Give your child 2 numbers of a fact family. Have them name the 3rd number and then name the corresponding facts.

Name _____

▶ Practice with Technology

Fact Families • Computer

Click on the ▮.

Click on Level 1.

Click on the open mat.

Find the 🐢 stamp.

Stamp out 8 🐢 and 7 🐢.

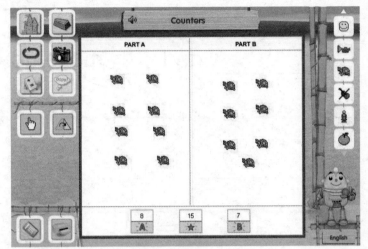

Add
8 + 7 = 15
7 + 8 = ____

Subtract
15 − 8 = 7
15 − 7 = ____

8, 7, and 15 make up this fact family.

Stamp out each fact family.

10. 6 + 5 = ____   ____ − ____ = ____

____ + ____ = ____   ____ − ____ = ____

____, ____, and ____ make up this fact family.

11.
____ + ____ = ____   16 − 7 = ____

____ + ____ = ____   ____ − ____ = ____

____, ____, and ____ make up this fact family.

Stamp out each fact family.

12. ___ + ___ = ___   ___ – ___ = ___

___ + ___ = ___   ___ – ___ = ___

____, ___, and ____ make up this fact family.

13. ___ + ___ = ___   ___ – ___ = ___

___ + ___ = ___   ___ – ___ = ___

___, ___, and ___ make up this fact family.

14. ___ + ___ = ___   ___ – ___ = ___

___ + ___ = ___   ___ – ___ = ___

___, ___, and ___ make up this fact family.

15. **WRITING IN ►MATH** What is a fact family?
Give an example of a fact family.

_____

‒ ‒ ‒ ‒ ‒ ‒ ‒ ‒ ‒ ‒ ‒ ‒ ‒ ‒ ‒ ‒ ‒ ‒ ‒ ‒

_____

‒ ‒ ‒ ‒ ‒ ‒ ‒ ‒ ‒ ‒ ‒ ‒ ‒ ‒ ‒ ‒ ‒ ‒ ‒ ‒

Math at Home Activity: Challenge your child to find all the fact families that make 15.

Name _____

Ways to Model Numbers

Get Ready

Main Idea

I will model a number in different ways.

There are many ways to make the same sum. Use counters.

Part	Part
●●●●	○○○○
●●●	○○○○
Whole	
15	

Part	Part
7	8
Whole	
15	

Part	Part
6	9
Whole	
15	

Part	Part
8	7
Whole	
15	

Part	Part
9	6
Whole	
15	

✓ Check

Use  and WorkMat 3.

1.

Part	Part
Whole	
16	

Part	Part
Whole	
16	

Part	Part
Whole	
16	

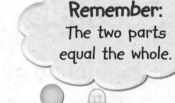 **Remember:** The two parts equal the whole.

2.

Part	Part
Whole	
14	

Part	Part
Whole	
14	

Part	Part
Whole	
14	

3. 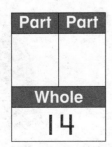 **Talk About It** Is there another way to make 16?

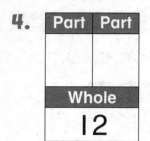

Use ⬤◯ and WorkMat 3.
Write ways to make the number.

4.

Part	Part
Whole	
12	

Part	Part
Whole	
12	

Part	Part
Whole	
12	

Part	Part
Whole	
12	

Part	Part
Whole	
12	

5.

Part	Part
Whole	
13	

Part	Part
Whole	
13	

Part	Part
Whole	
13	

Part	Part
Whole	
13	

Part	Part
Whole	
13	

Write the missing part.

6.

Part	Part
7	
Whole	
16	

Part	Part
9	
Whole	
15	

Part	Part
7	
Whole	
14	

Part	Part
4	
Whole	
13	

Part	Part
8	
Whole	
12	

Data File

Michigan has many places to enjoy water sports. One thing to do is a boat race.

7. On Monday, there were 8 girls signed up for the race. On Tuesday, there were double that number. How many girls were signed up on Tuesday?

_____ girls

Math at Home Activity: Give your child a number and have them give you the other names for that number.

Write a number sentence to show how many white and red stripes are on the flag.

_____ + _____ = _____

Problem Solving in Social Studies

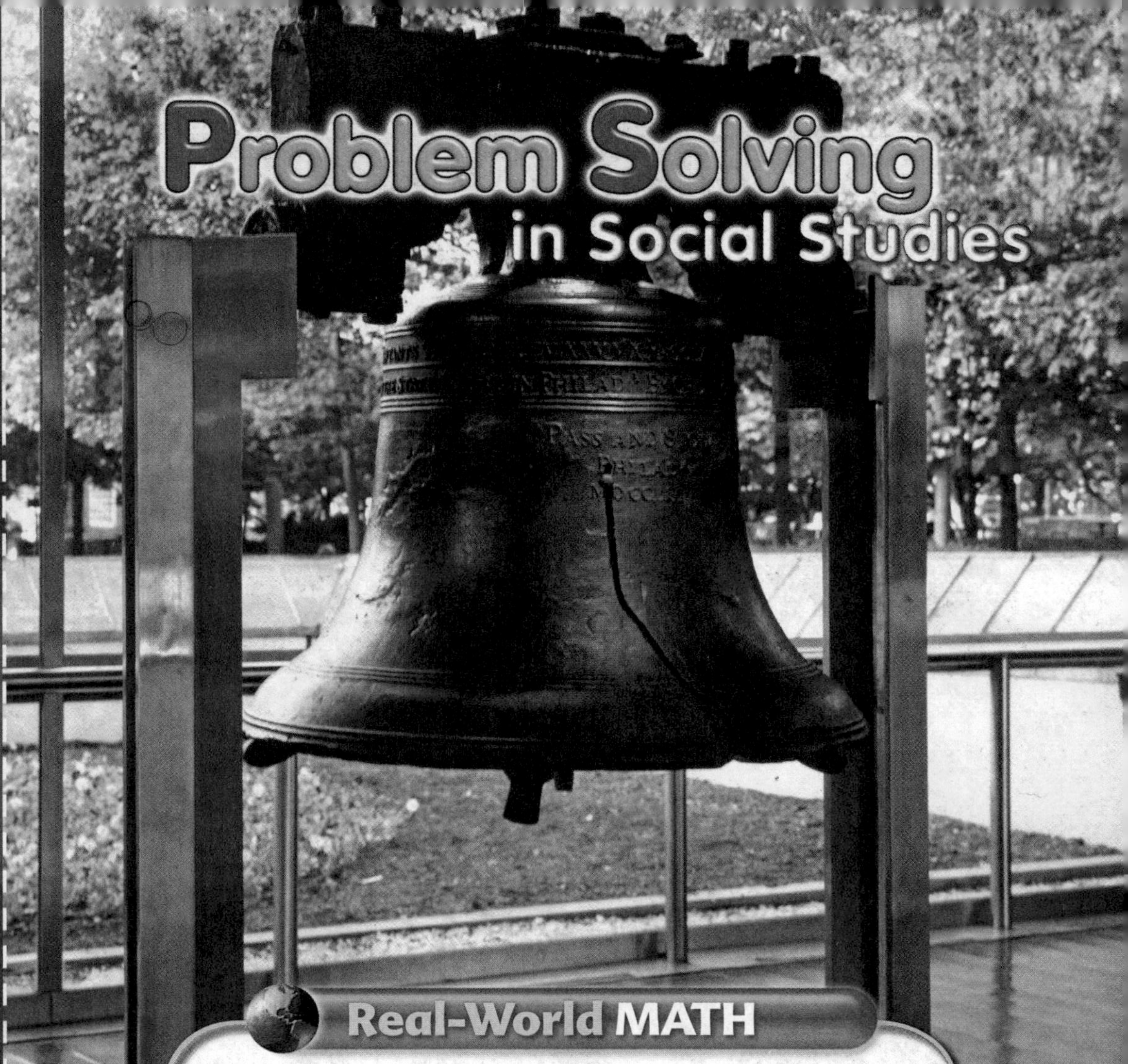

Real-World MATH

Each year, many people visit American symbols. This is the Liberty Bell. It is in Pennsylvania.

This book belongs to

_____

A

This is the Statue of Liberty. It is in New York.

18 first grade students saw the Statue of Liberty today. 4 saw it before lunch. How many saw it after lunch?

_____ students

This is Mount Rushmore. It is in South Dakota.

What other American symbols can you think of?

Name _____

Vocabulary

1. Circle the answer that shows a fact family.

a.	b.
7 + 4 = 11	6 + 5 = 11
4 + 7 = 11	5 + 6 = 11
11 − 4 = 7	4 + 6 = 11
11 − 7 = 4	6 + 4 = 11

Concepts

Draw the missing dots to show a double.
Write the doubles fact.

2.

____ + ____ = 16

3.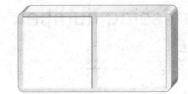

____ + ____ = 12

Draw the counters. Then add.

4.

9 + 2 = ____ , because

9 + 1 + 1 = ____ and

____ + 1 = ____

5.

9 + 4 = ____ , because

9 + 1 + 3 = ____ and

____ + 3 = ____

Complete the fact family.

6.

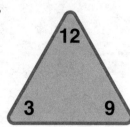

9 + 3 = _____   12 − 3 = _____

3 + 9 = _____   12 − 9 = _____

Add the doubles. Then subtract.

7.   7   14   8. 2 + 2 = _____
    + 7   − 7
    _____   _____   4 − 2 = _____

Find each missing number.

9. 12 − 5 = _____   10. 14 − 9 = _____

   5 + _____ = 12   9 + _____ = 14

Write ways to make the number.

11.

Part	Part
Whole	
15	

Part	Part
Whole	
15	

Part	Part
Whole	
15	

Problem Solving

12. Adam hung 8 pictures in two rows.
    He hung 4 pictures in the top row.
    How many did he hang in the bottom row?   _____

Summative Assessment

Name _____

Listen as your teacher reads each problem.
Choose the correct answer.

1.

○　　　　　　　　○

○　　　　　　　　○

4.　[7 + 5 = 12]

7 − 5 = 2　　　12 − 7 = 5
○　　　　　　　　○

12 − 12 = 0　　5 − 2 = 3
○　　　　　　　　○

2.　[11 − 7 = 4]

11 − 4 = 7　　7 − 4 = 3
○　　　　　　　　○

4 − 4 = 0　　11 − 0 = 11
○　　　　　　　　○

5.　[3 + 7 = 10]

6 + 4　　　　　11 − 2
○　　　　　　　　○

3 + 6　　　　　5 + 4
○　　　　　　　　○

3.　[16　36　12　24]

○　36　24　16　12
○　16　36　12　24
○　12　16　24　36
○　24　12　36　16

6.　[30　40　50　60]

61　　　　　　　65
○　　　　　　　　○

70　　　　　　　80
○　　　　　　　　○

7.

◯ ◯

◯ ◯

8.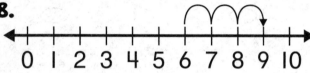

8   9   10   12

◯ ◯ ◯ ◯

9.
$$3$$
$$7$$
$$+\ 1$$

3   9

◯   ◯

10   11

◯   ◯

10.

$8 + 4 = 12$ $6 + 6 = 12$

◯   ◯

$5 + 5 = 10$ $4 + 4 = 8$

◯   ◯

11. Ty found 6 shells.
Louis found 8 shells.
How many did they find
in all?

_____ shells

12. Jade has 13 stars.
She gave some to Kei.
Now she has 8 left.
How many stars did Jade
give Kei?

_____ stars

Summative Assessment

Identify Coins

Key Vocabulary
penny 1¢
nickel 5¢
dime 10¢
quarter 25¢

30¢

Explore
Each flower costs 30¢. How much would 2 flowers cost?

_____¢

Mitch Diamond/Index Stock Imagery

Name ______________________

Math Online
Take the Chapter Readiness Quiz at macmillanmh.com.

Are You Ready for Chapter 11?

1. Skip count by 5s.

5, 10, ____, ____, ____, ____

2. Skip count by 10s.

10, 20, ____, ____, ____, ____

3. Circle all the pennies.
Mark an X on the nickels.

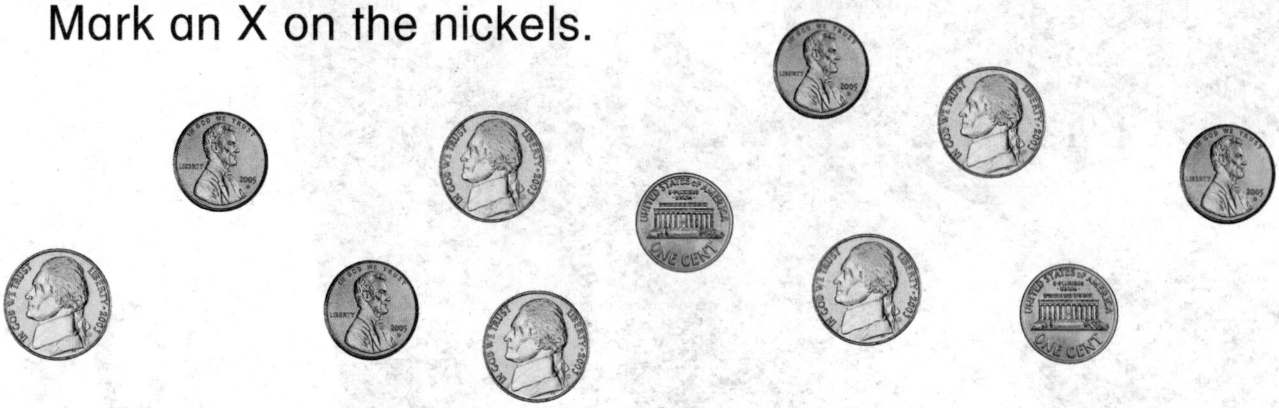

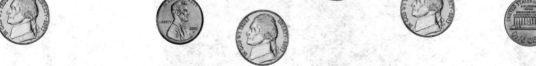

4. Kimi is counting her gloves. She skip counts by twos. She counts up to 12. How many pairs of gloves does Kimi have? _____ pairs

5. There are 3 vases. Each vase has 10 flowers. How many flowers in all? _____ flowers

This page checks skills needed for Chapter 11.

MATH at HOME

Dear Family,
Today my class started Chapter 11, **Identify Coins**. In this chapter, I will learn to identify and count coins. Here is an activity we can do and a list of books we can read together.

Love, _____

Activity

Set up a store. Put price tags on items around the house. Give your child coins to practice counting out the change to buy the items.

Key Vocabulary

penny 1¢   **nickel** 5¢

dime 10¢   **quarter** 25¢

Math Online > Click on the eGlossary link at macmillanmh.com to find out more about these words. There are 13 languages.

Books to Read

The Three Silly Billies
by Margie Palatini
Simon & Schuster Children's
Publishing, 2005.

The Penny Pot
by Stuart J. Murphy
Harper Trophy
Publishers, 1998.

The Coin Counting Book
Rozanne Lanczak Williams
Charlesbridge
Publishing, 2001.

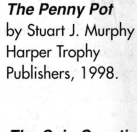

MATEMÁTICAS en CASA

Estimada familia:

Hoy mi clase comenzó el Capítulo 11, **Identifica monedas.** En este capítulo, aprenderé a identificar y a contar monedas. A continuación, hay una actividad que podemos hacer y una lista de libros que podemos leer juntos.

Cariños, _____

Actividad

Organicen una tienda. Coloquen etiquetas de precios en objetos alrededor de la casa. Denle monedas a su hijo(a) a fin de que las cuente para comprar los objetos.

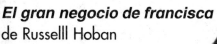

Vocabulario clave

un centavo 1¢   **cinco centavos** 5¢

diez centavos 10¢ **veinticinco centavos** 25¢

Math Online ▸ Visiten el enlace eGlossary en macmillanmh.com para averiguar más sobre estas palabras, las cuales se muestran en 13 idiomas.

Libros recomendados

El gran negocio de francisca
de Russelll Hoban
Harper Trophy, 1996 .

De compras con mamá
de Mercer Mayer
Golden Books, 1997.

Matematicas y dinero
de Susan Ring
Yellow Umbrella Books, 2005.

Name _____

Pennies and Nickels

Get Ready

Main Idea

I will count pennies and nickels.

Vocabulary

penny

nickel

cent (¢)

> Start counting with the coin of greater value.

You can count **pennies** and **nickels**.

 or
penny

 or
nickel

> 5 pennies equal 1 nickel, so I could trade 1 nickel for 5 pennies.

1¢ = 1 **cent**   5¢ = 5 **cents**

Count by fives to count the nickels.
Then, count on by ones
to count the pennies.

5 ¢ **10** ¢ **11** ¢ **12** ¢ **13** ¢

Check

Use  to circle each penny.
Count the coins. Write each price on the tag.

1.

_____ ¢   _____ ¢   _____ ¢   _____ ¢

2.

_____ ¢   _____ ¢   _____ ¢   _____ ¢   _____ ¢

3. **Talk About It** My friend wants to give me 1 nickel for
10 pennies. Is that a fair trade? Explain.

Use  to circle each penny. Count the coins.
Write each price on the tag.

4.

_____¢ _____¢ _____¢ _____¢ _____¢

5.

_____¢ _____¢ _____¢ _____¢

6.

_____¢ _____¢ _____¢ _____¢

7.

_____¢ _____¢ _____¢ _____¢ _____¢

8.

_____¢ _____¢ _____¢ _____¢

Problem Solving

9. Critical Thinking Mindy has 8 pennies.
How much money does she have? _____¢
Draw coins to show that same amount a different way.

Math at Home Activity: Give your child an amount of money to show using pennies and nickels.

Name _____

Pennies and Dimes

Get Ready

Main Idea

I will count pennies and dimes.

Vocabulary

dime

I have 32¢.

or

dime

10¢ = ten cents

Count by tens to count dimes.

10¢   20¢   30¢   31¢   32¢

10 pennies equal 1 dime.

Check

Use ✏ crayon to circle the dimes. Count the coins.
Write how much in all.

1.

____¢ ____¢ ____¢ ____¢
                   in all

2.

____¢ ____¢ ____¢ ____¢
                   in all

3.

____¢ ____¢ ____¢ ____¢ ____¢ ____¢ ____¢ ____¢
                                        in all

4. **Talk About It** How many dimes are the same as 50 pennies?

Remember
Start counting with
the coin of
greater value.

Use ◄━ crayon ━► to circle the dimes.
Count the coins. Write how much in all.

5.

_____¢ _____¢ _____¢

_____¢
in all

6.

_____¢ _____¢ _____¢ _____¢ _____¢ _____¢

_____¢
in all

7.

_____¢ _____¢ _____¢ _____¢

_____¢
in all

8.

_____¢ _____¢ _____¢ _____¢ _____¢ _____¢

_____¢
in all

9.

_____¢ _____¢ _____¢ _____¢ _____¢

_____¢
in all

H.O.T. Problem

10. Thinking Math

You have 3 coins. They equal 20 cents.
Draw the coins you have.

 Math at Home Activity: Give your child 3 dimes; ask him or her how many pennies that equals.

Name _____

Pennies, Nickels, and Dimes

Hands-On Activity

Get Ready

Main Idea

I will count pennies, nickels, and dimes.

Pennies, nickels, and dimes have different values.

I have 2 dimes, 1 nickel, and 3 pennies.

You can use different coins to make 10¢.		
1 dime	2 nickels	10 pennies

10¢ 20¢ 25¢ 26¢ 27¢ 28¢

Check

Use coins.

You have these coins.	Draw the coins. Show how you count them.	How much money?
1.  1 3 1	(10¢) (5¢) (5¢) (5¢) (1¢) 10¢ 15¢ 20¢ 25¢ 26¢	26¢
2. 0 2 4	___¢ ___¢ ___¢ ___¢ ___¢ ___¢	___¢

3. **Talk About It** Describe the relationship among a penny, a nickel, and a dime.

Use coins.

	You have these coins.	Draw the coins. Show how you count them.	How much money?
4.	4 0 2	____¢ ____¢ ____¢ ____¢ ____¢ ____¢	_____¢
5.	2 2 1	____¢ ____¢ ____¢ ____¢ ____¢	_____¢
6.	5 1 0	____¢ ____¢ ____¢ ____¢ ____¢ ____¢	_____¢
7.	1 1 4	____¢ ____¢ ____¢ ____¢ ____¢ ____¢	_____¢

Problem Solving

8. Logical Reasoning You have pennies, nickels, and dimes.

You pick up 3 of those coins.

What is the greatest amount of money you could have? _____ ¢

What is the least amount of money you could have? _____ ¢

Math at Home Activity: Give your child some pennies, nickels, and dimes. Have him/her count the value of the group.

Name _____

Counting Money

Get Ready

Main Idea

I will count mixed sets of coins.

When you count pennies, nickels, and dimes, start with the coin that has the greatest value.

I am going to the fair. I need 37¢ for a ticket. Circle how much money I need for my ticket.

Check

Circle how much money you need.
Use coins. Count.

1.

ADMISSION TICKET
Admit One
28¢

Draw how much money you need.

2.

25¢

3. **Talk About It** How are 20 pennies, 4 nickels, and 2 dimes alike?

Circle how much money you need.

4.

 16¢

Draw how much money you need.

5.

 19¢

6.

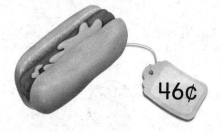 46¢

Problem Solving

7. Logical Reasoning A balloon costs 23¢.
You have 2 dimes, 1 nickel, and 2 pennies.
Do you have enough money? Explain.

_____

_____

_____

_____

358 three hundred fifty-eight

Math at Home Activity: Give your child a price (such as 33¢) and have him/her describe what combination of coins he/she could use to make that amount.

Name _____

Problem-Solving Strategy
Act it Out

Main Idea

I will act it out to solve a problem.

Peg bought a box of pencils.
The pencils cost 13¢.
Peg has 2 nickels.
What other coins does
she need?

Understand

What do I know? Underline what you know.

What do I need to find? Circle the question.

Plan

How will I solve the problem?

I can use coins to act out the problem.

Solve

Act it out.

Show .

Count and show the coins
needed to make 13¢.

Check

Look back.

Is my answer reasonable?

Try It

Act it out to solve.

1. Cliff wants to buy a hat.
   It costs 40¢. He has 25¢.
   What other coins does he need?

Cliff needs _____.

2. Rina wants to buy a doll for 10 cents.
   Which coins could she use?

Rina could use _____.

Your Turn

Act it out to solve.

3. Carla wants a fruit bar.
   The fruit bar costs 30 cents.
   Carla has 1 dime.
   How many more dimes does she need?

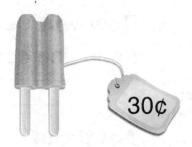

Carla needs _____ dimes.

4. Jeremy wants to buy 2 fish.
   The fish are 5 cents each.
   What coins could he use
   to buy the fish?

Jeremy could use _____.

Math at Home Activity: Use household items to set up a make believe store in your home. Put prices on each item. Give your child pennies, nickels, and dimes to use to buy items in the store.

Name _____

Circle the pennies. Count.

1.

_____¢ _____¢ _____¢ _____¢

_____¢
in all

2.

_____¢ _____¢ _____¢ _____¢ _____¢ _____¢

_____¢
in all

Circle how much money you need.

3.

ADMISSION TICKET
Admit One
35¢

NOW PLAYING

4.

ADMISSION TICKET
Admit One
26¢

5. A balloon costs 23¢. You have
Can you buy it? Explain.

_____

- - - - - - - - - - - - - - - - - - -

_____

Put an X on the ones you take away.
Write how many are left.

6.

   10 take away 3 is _____.

7.

   9 take away 3 is _____.

Skip count by 2s or 5s.

8. 2, _____, 6, _____, 10, 12, 14

9. 5, 10, _____, _____, 25, 30

Use [cube] to measure.

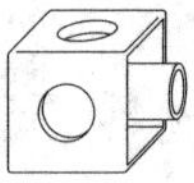

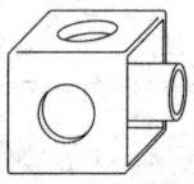

10.

   about _____ [cube]

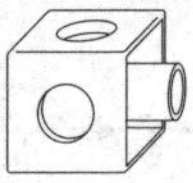

11.

   about _____ [cube]

12.

   about _____ [cube]

Formative Assessment

Name _____

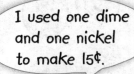
Equal Amounts

Get Ready

Main Idea

I will show different ways to make the same amount of money.

You can show the same amount of money in more than one way.

I used two nickels and five pennies to make 15¢.

I used one dime and one nickel to make 15¢.

One Way

Another Way

Check

Use coins. Show each amount a different way.

1. Show 23¢.

One Way	Another Way

2. Show 18¢.

One Way	Another Way

3. **Talk About It** Tell the ways you can show 10¢.

Use coins. Show each amount a different way.

4. Show 37¢.

One Way	Another Way

5. Show 40¢.

One Way	Another Way

6. Show 51¢.

One Way	Another Way

7. ◖ **WRITING IN** ▶**MATH** Write a number story about these coins. Ask a friend to solve the problem.

_____

_____

_____

_____

Math at Home Activity: Use coins to make an amount of money less than $1.00. Have your child make that same amount another way.

Name _____

Quarters

Get Ready

Main Idea

I will count pennies, nickels, dimes, and quarters.

Vocabulary

quarter

A **quarter** is worth 25 cents.

 or

quarter

25¢ = 25 cents

25¢	25¢	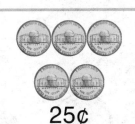 25¢

Count. Start with the quarter.

 25¢   **35**¢   **40**¢   **41**¢   **42**¢

Check

Remember
Start counting with the coin of greatest value.

Count. Write the price.

1.

Price

_____¢ _____¢ _____¢ _____¢ _____¢   _____¢

Draw coins to show the price.

2.

 37¢

---

3. **Talk About It** Which is worth more: a quarter or 2 dimes? How do you know?

Count. Write the price.

4.

Price

_____¢ _____¢ _____¢ _____¢ _____¢   _____¢

5.

Price

_____¢ _____¢ _____¢ _____¢ _____¢ _____¢   _____¢

Draw coins to show the price.

6.

7.

8.

q.

Chapter 11   Lesson 7

Name _____

> **Practice** **with Technology**

Quarters • Computer

Use the tool chest.

Click on Level 1.

Click on the open mat.

- Stamp out 1 quarter.
- Stamp out 4 dimes.
- Stamp out 3 nickels.

10. Draw the coins.
Write the amount.

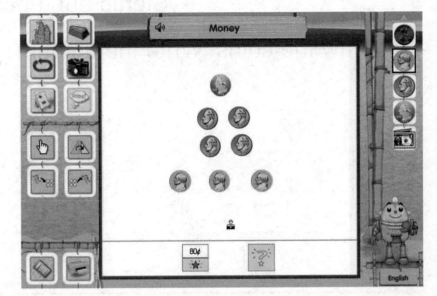

Money

80¢

_80_ ¢

Use the tool chest.

Click on Level 1.

Click on the open mat.

- Stamp out 5 dimes.
- Stamp out 1 nickel.
- Stamp out 4 pennies.

11. Draw the coins. Write the amount.

_____ ¢

Click on the tool chest. Click on Level 1.
Click on the open mat.

- Stamp out 2 quarters.
- Stamp out 1 nickel.
- Stamp out 4 pennies.

12. Draw the coins. Write the amount.

_____ ¢

Data File

Every year New Jersey has a hot
air balloon festival. The festival has
music, games, and balloon rides.

13. Pretend you have these coins
to spend.

How much money do you have? _____ ¢

Math at Home Activity: Find items under $1.00 in an advertisement.
Have your child tell you the coins needed to buy each item.

Name _____

Problem-Solving Investigation

I have a pocket full of coins.
They total 66 cents.
I have at least 1 penny, 1 nickel,
1 dime, and 1 quarter.
What coins do I have?

Main Idea

I will choose a strategy to solve a problem.

Your Mission:
Find which coins total 66 cents.

Understand

What do I know? Underline what you know.

What do I need to find? Circle it.

Plan

How will I solve the problem?

One way is to guess and check.

Solve

I could have 1 penny, 1 nickel, 1 dime, and 1 quarter.
   That is only 41¢, not 66¢.

I could have 1 penny, 1 nickel, 2 dimes, and 2 quarters.
   That is 76¢, not 66¢.

I could have 1 penny, 1 nickel, 1 dime, and 2 quarters.
   That is 66¢!

Check

Look back.

Is my answer reasonable?

Problem-Solving
Strategies

• Guess and check
• Act it out
• Make a table

Choose a strategy. Solve.

1. Edwin has all dimes in his piggy bank.
He counted the money.
It totals 50 cents. How many
dimes does he have?

_____ dimes

2. Larry and Ruthie each have 25 cents.
Larry has a quarter. Ruthie has 3 coins.
What coins does Ruthie have?

_____

_____

3. Ivan has 2 quarters and 1 dime.
How much money does he have?

_____ cents

4. Turtles are 10 cents at the pet store.
Derek wants 4 turtles. How much money
does he need?

_____ cents

Math at Home Activity: Take advantage of problem-solving
opportunities during daily routines such as riding in the car, bedtime,
doing laundry, putting away groceries, planning schedules, and so on.

Name _____

Money Amounts

Main Idea

I will compare the value of a set of coins with prices.

Counting coins helps you know if you have enough money to buy something.

This ball costs 42¢.

Here are your coins:

How much money did you count?

$\underline{42}$ ¢

Do you have enough money?

(Yes)   No

Check

Look at the price	Count the coins	Do you have enough money?
1. CHALK **37¢**		Yes No
2. COLORING BOOK **53¢**		Yes No

3.  **Talk About It** A ride costs 50¢. Manuel has 3 quarters. Nadine has 4 dimes. Who has enough money for the ride? Explain?

Look at the price	Count the coins	Do you have enough money?
4. 61¢		Yes No
5. 48¢		Yes No
6. 55¢		Yes No
7. 27¢		Yes No

Problem Solving

8. Logical Reasoning Ling has 50¢. He has 2 of the same kind of coin in his hand. What coin does he have? _____

Math at Home Activity: Find an item in the store that costs less then $1.00. Have your child describe two combinations of coins that could be used to buy that item.

Name _____

Count the coins. Circle all of the toys you have
enough money to buy.

 34¢

 67¢

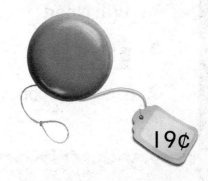 19¢

1.      kite   plane   yo-yo

2.    kite   plane   yo-yo

3.    kite   plane   yo-yo

4.    kite   plane   yo-yo

5.    kite   plane   yo-yo

Extra
Practice

Game Time

Who Has More?
Money

You Will Need

- 🎲 🎲
- pencil and paper

Play with a partner.
- Roll the 🎲.
- Find the picture that matches the number you rolled.
- The person with more money gets a point.
- Keep a tally chart.
- The first player to 10 points wins!

0      0   

1      1   

2      2   

3      3   

4      4   

5      5

D

What would you sell at a yard sale? Draw the items on the table. Do not forget the price tags!

FOLD DOWN

Problem Solving
in Social Studies

Yard Sale Today

Real-World MATH

Sometimes people buy new things. Sometimes people buy used things. Yard sales are filled with all kinds of used things.

This book belongs to

_____

A

Jake has ten pennies, two dimes, and 3 nickels. Can Jake buy the puzzle? ___

5¢

25¢

$1

75¢

20¢

50¢

30¢

Sandy has two dimes and a nickel. What can she buy? ___

Luis has 5 pennies. What can he buy? ___

Name _____

Vocabulary

Circle the picture that matches the word.

1. **cent**	2. **penny**	3. **nickel**
¢ $		

4. **dime**	5. **quarter**

Concepts

Count to find each price. Write each price on the tag.

6.

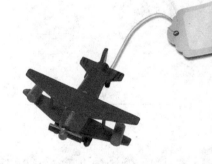

_____¢_____¢_____¢_____ ¢

7.

_____¢_____¢_____¢_____¢_____¢_____ ¢

Circle how much money you need.

8.

35¢

Show the same amount of money a different way.

9. Show 27¢.

One Way	Another Way

10. Count the coins to find the price.
Write the price.

     Price

_____¢ _____¢ _____¢ _____¢ _____¢ _____¢

Problem Solving

11. How can you make 40¢ using the fewest coins?
Explain.

_____

_ _ _ _ _ _ _ _ _ _ _ _ _ _ _ _ _ _ _

_____

Summative Assessment

Name _____

Listen as your teacher reads the problem.
Choose the correct answer.

1.

⬭   ⬭

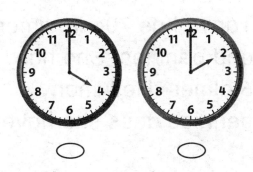

⬭   ⬭

2.

3¢   11¢   21¢   30¢

⬭   ⬭   ⬭   ⬭

3.

⬭

⬭

⬭

⬭

4.

⬭   ⬭

⬭   ⬭

Chapter 11   three hundred seventy-nine   **379**

5.

$$6 + 4 = 10$$

$10 - 6 = 10$ ○ $6 - 2 = 4$ ○

$6 - 4 = 2$ ○ $4 + 6 = 10$ ○

6.   18 ○   20 ○   22 ○   27 ○

7.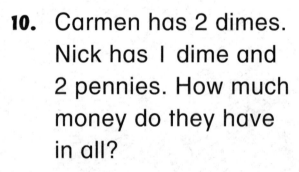

4¢ ○   8¢ ○   12¢ ○   20¢ ○

8.

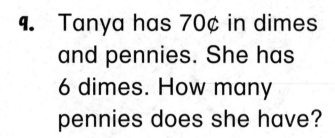

21	22	23	24	25	26	27	28	29	30
31	32	33	34	35	36	37	38	39	40
41	42	43	44	45	46	47	48	49	50

24 ○   33 ○   34 ○   40 ○

9. Tanya has 70¢ in dimes and pennies. She has 6 dimes. How many pennies does she have?

_____ pennies

10. Carmen has 2 dimes. Nick has 1 dime and 2 pennies. How much money do they have in all?

_____ ¢

Summative Assessment

Identify Geometric Figures

Key Vocabulary

sphere

rectangular prism

face

corner

Explore

Find objects in the classroom that look like these figures.

Name _____

Are You Ready for Chapter 12?

Circle the ⬭ figure.
Underline the △ figure.
Put an X on the ◯ figure.

1.

Put an X on the same figure.

2.

3.

4.

5.

6. Put an X on the figure that is inside the box.

This page checks skills needed for Chapter 12.

MATH at HOME

Dear Family,

Today my class started Chapter 12, **Identify Geometric Figures**. In this chapter, I will learn about three-dimensional and two-dimensional figures. I will also learn how to locate objects. Here is an activity we can do and a list of books we can read together.

Love,

_____

Activity

Have your child tell you the shape of road signs while you are driving. Look for triangles, rectangles, squares, and circles.

Key Vocabulary

corner point where lines, edges, or sides of a shape meet

position tell where an object is

Math Online Click on the eGlossary link at macmillanmh.com to find out more about these words. There are 13 languages.

Books to Read

Cubes, Cones, Cylinders, and Spheres
by Tana Hoban
Greenwillow, 2000.

If You Were a Preposition
by Nancy Loewen
Picture Willow
Books, 2006.

Shapes, Shapes, Shapes
by Tana Hoban
Greenwillow, 1986.

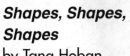

Estimada familia,

Hoy mi clase comenzó el Capítulo 12, **Identifica figuras geométricas**. En este capítulo, aprenderé acerca de las figuras sólidas, las formas y los mapas. A continuación, hay una actividad que podemos hacer y una lista de libros que podemos leer juntos.

Cariños,

_____

Actividad

Al andar en el auto, pídanle a su hijo(a) que les diga la forma que tienen las señales de tránsito. Busquen triángulos, rectángulos, cuadrados y círculos.

Vocabulario clave

esquina el punto donde se juntan las rectas, las artistas o los lados de una figura

posición dónde se localiza algo

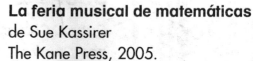

Math Online Visiten el enlace eGlossary en macmillanmh.com para averiguar más sobre estas palabras, las cuales se muestran en 13 idiomas.

Libros recomendados

Teo descubre las Formas
de Violeta Denou
Timun Mas, 1995

La feria musical de matemáticas
de Sue Kassirer
The Kane Press, 2005.

Ensamblando figuras geométricas
de Daneille Carroll
Yellow Umbrella books, 2006

Three-Dimensional Figures

Get Ready

Main Idea

I will identify three-dimensional figures.

Vocabulary

pyramid
cube
sphere
cone
cylinder
rectangular prism

Solid shapes are also called three-dimensional figures.

pyramid

cube

sphere

cone

cylinder

rectangular prism

Check

Look at the three-dimensional figure. Circle the objects with the same shape.

1.

cylinder

2.

cone

3.

pyramid

4.

rectangular prism

5. **Talk About It** How is a rectangular prism like your math book?

Find an object in your classroom that matches each three-dimensional figure. Draw the object.

6.

rectangular prism

7.

cylinder

8.

cone

9.

sphere

10.

cube

11.

pyramid

12. ✏️ **WRITING IN** ▶**MATH** Sort the objects into two groups.
Circle each object in one group green.
Circle each object in the other group blue.

Explain your sorting rule.

_____

_ _ _ _ _ _ _ _ _ _ _ _ _ _ _ _ _ _ _ _

_____

_ _ _ _ _ _ _ _ _ _ _ _ _ _ _ _ _ _ _ _

 Math at Home Activity: Have your child find objects at home that have the same shape as the three-dimensional figures above.

Name _____

Faces and Corners

Get Ready

Main Idea

I will identify faces and corners of three-dimensional figures.

Vocabulary

face

corner

Three-dimensional figures have faces and corners.
The **face** is the flat side.
The **corner** (vertex) is where the faces meet.

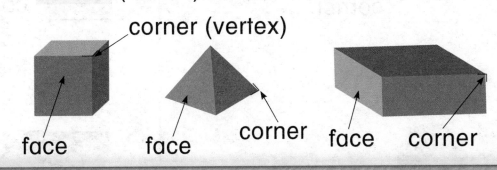

corner (vertex)

face   face   corner   face   corner

Check

Use three-dimensional figures to help.
Circle all the three-dimensional figures that match the rule.

1. 8 corners

2. 5 faces

3. 0 corners

4. 6 faces

5. ⟨Talk About It⟩ How is a cube different from a sphere?

Use three-dimensional figures to help.
Write how many.

6.

_____ corner

_____ face

7.

_____ corners

_____ faces

8.

_____ corners

_____ faces

9.

_____ corners

_____ faces

Problem Solving

10. **Visual Thinking** How are these three-dimensional figures alike? How are they different?

  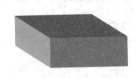

_____

_ _

_____

_ _

_____

Math at Home Activity: Help your child find three-dimensional figures at home and then identify the faces and corners.

Problem-Solving Strategy
Look for a Pattern

Main Idea

I will look for a pattern to solve a problem.

Marcus made a pattern with his blocks. Which block is missing?

Understand

What do I know?
Underline what you know.
What do I need to find?
Circle the question.

Plan

How will I solve the problem?

I will look for a pattern.

Solve

Look for a pattern.
Circle the pattern unit.
Draw the block that is missing.

Check

Look back.
Is my answer reasonable?

Try It

Look for a pattern to solve.

1. June made a line of blocks. Draw the block that is missing.

2. These are Quinn's blocks. Draw the block that is missing.

Your Turn

Look for a pattern to solve.

3. Ayden made a line of blocks. Draw the block that is missing.

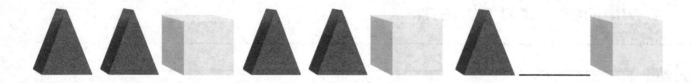

4. Grace is making a line of blocks. She needs 2 more blocks to finish. Draw the blocks that are missing.

 Math at Home Activity: Look for patterns on the boxes and cans of food items. Ask your child what comes next.

Name _____

Two- and Three-Dimensional Figures

Get Ready

Main Idea

I will match faces of two- and three-dimensional figures.

The face of a three-dimensional figure is a two-dimensional figure.

The face of this cone is a circle.

✓ Check

Use three-dimensional figures. Trace one face.
Circle the shape that matches.

1.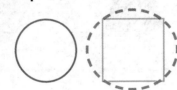

2. △ ○

Circle the three-dimensional figure you could trace to make each shape.

3.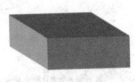

4. △

5. **Talk About It** How are a cone and a cylinder alike?
How are they different?

Look at the two-dimensional figure.
Circle the objects that have the same face.

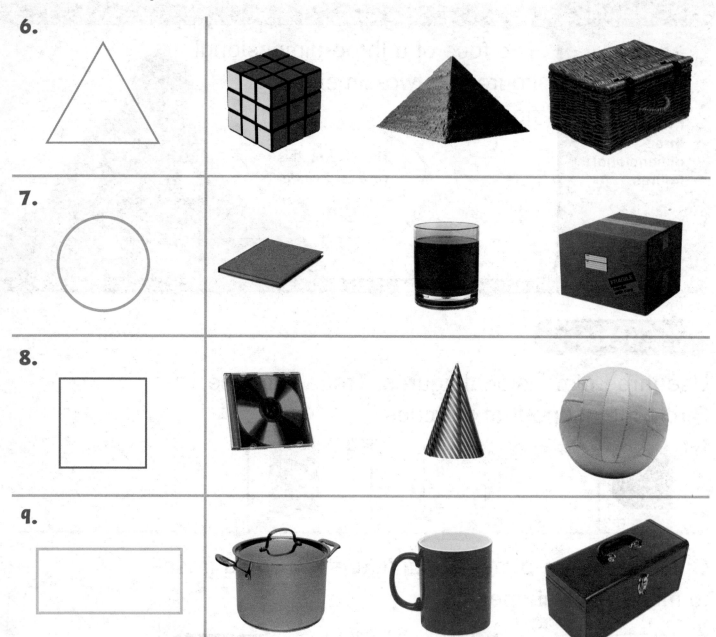

6.

7.

8.

9.

Problem Solving

10. Critical Thinking Name a three-dimensional figure
that has faces with more than 1 two-dimensional figure.

_ _

Math at Home Activity: Have your child trace around objects
found at home to make triangles, squares, rectangles, and circles.

Name _____

Look at the three-dimensional figures. Color the shape in the castle that matches the three-dimensional figure.

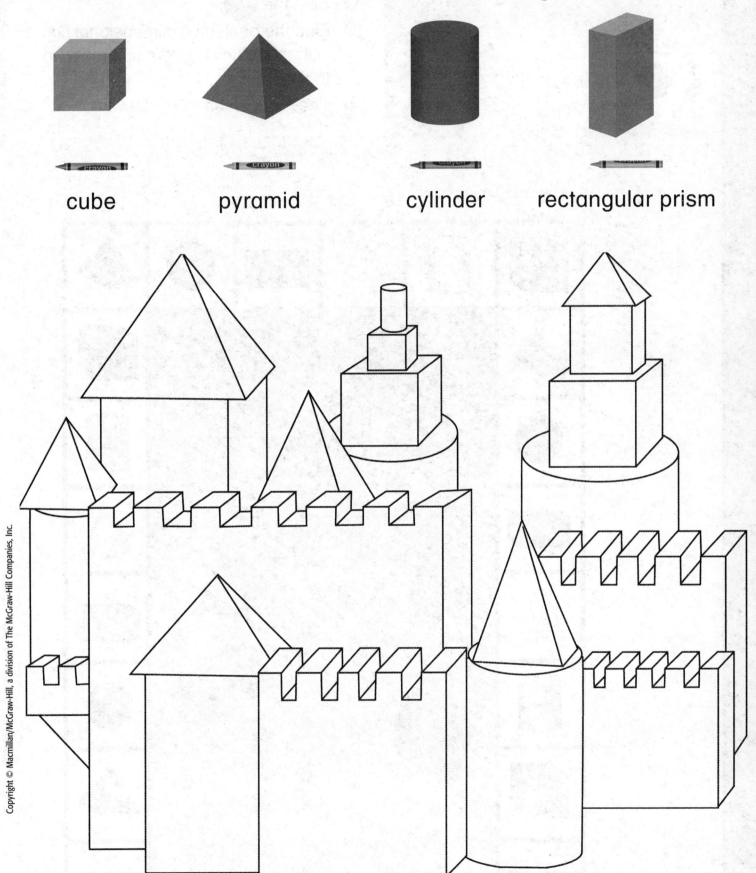

cube   pyramid   cylinder   rectangular prism

Game Time

Corners
Three-Dimensional Figures

Play with a partner. Take turns.
- Spin the 🔵.
- Find the next three-dimensional figure with that many corners and move to that space.
- The first person to Finish wins!

You Will Need

  with 0, 1, 5, 8

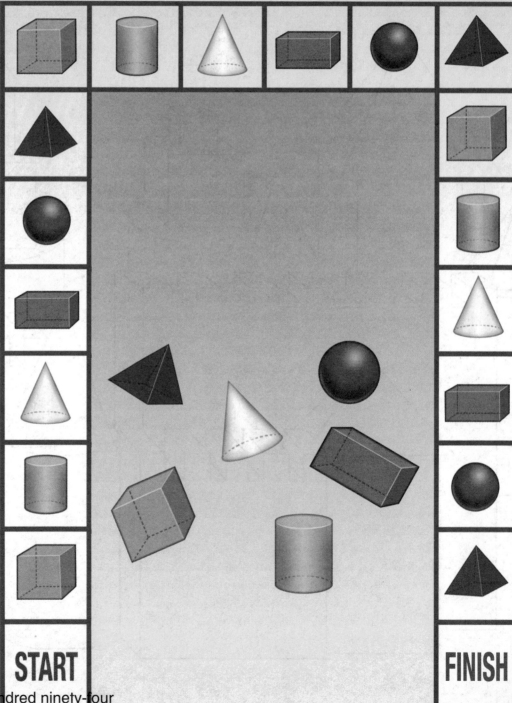

START

FINISH

Name _____

Two-Dimensional Figures

Get Ready

Main Idea

I will identify and describe two-dimensional figures.

Vocabulary

triangle
rectangle
square
circle
side

Review Vocabulary

corner

Flat figures are called two-dimensional figures. Some two-dimensional figures have straight sides and corners.

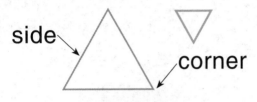

triangles

rectangles

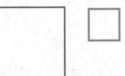

squares

circles

✓ Check

Write how many.

1.

_____ sides

_____ corners

2.

_____ sides

_____ corners

3.

_____ sides

_____ corners

4.

_____ sides

_____ corners

5. What objects in your classroom are the shape of a circle?

Practice

> **Remember**
> Squares, circles, triangles, and rectangles can be different sizes.

6. Draw a picture. Use , 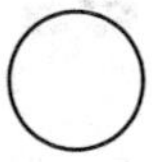, 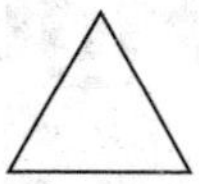, and 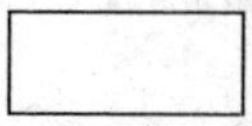.

Color 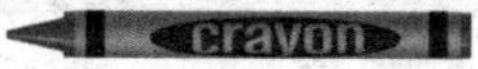
crayon

Color 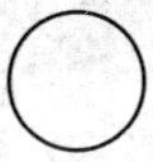 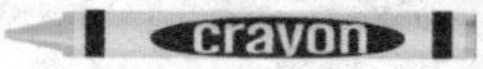
crayon

Color 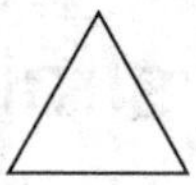 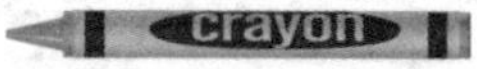
crayon

Color 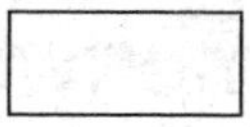 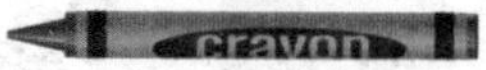
crayon

H.O.T. Problem

7. Explaining Math How is a square different from a rectangle?

____

____

Math at Home Activity: Have your child identify and describe two-dimensional figures in your home or neighborhood.

Name _____

Draw an object that matches each three-dimensional figure.

1.

rectangular
prism

2.

cylinder

Circle all the three-dimensional figures that match the rule.

3. 8 **corners**

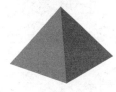

4. 5 **faces**

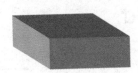

Circle the object that has a face with the same shape.
Look at the two-dimensional shape.

5.

 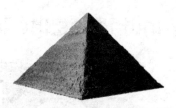 

Circle the answer.

6. I have 4 corners.
I have 2 long sides
and 2 short sides.
What am I?

 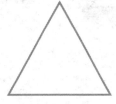

Spiral Review   Chapters 1–12

Write each missing number.

7. 11 – 6 = _____

6 + _____ = 11

8. 13 – 5 = _____

5 + _____ = 13

9. 12 – 5 = _____

5 + _____ = 12

10. Show 39¢.

39¢

Add.

11. 2 + 6 = _____

12. 8 + 2 = _____

13. 1 + 4 = _____

14. 3 + 6 = _____

15. Circle the activity that takes the least amount of time.

half hour   four hours   one hour

Formative Assessment

Name _____

Problem-Solving Investigation

Main Idea

I will choose a strategy to solve a problem.

Your Mission:
Find the shape that is described.

The window in my room has 4 sides and 4 corners. Each side is the same length.
What shape is the window?

Understand

What do I know?
Underline what you know.
What do I need to find?
Circle it.

Plan

How will I solve the problem?
One way is to draw a picture.

Remember the window has 4 sides.

Solve

Draw a picture.
Use the clues to draw a picture.

Check

Look back.
Is my answer resonable?

Copyright © Macmillan/McGraw-Hill, a division of The McGraw-Hill Companies, Inc.

Problem-Solving Strategies

- Draw a picture
- Find a pattern
- Use logical reasoning

Choose a strategy. Solve.

1. Ramón's toy box is a rectangular prism. How many corners does it have?

_____ corners

2. LaToya is buying a picture frame. She wants the frame to have 4 corners and all the sides the same length. What should the shape of the frame be?

_____

3. Katie first puts a red bead, then a blue bead, and then a yellow bead on a string. She starts with a square bead. The next bead is a triangle. What color is the triangle?

_____

4. Beatriz is drawing a pattern. The first triangle points up, the next points down, the third points up, the next points down. Which way is the 8th triangle pointing?

_____

Math at Home Activity: Take advantage of problem-solving opportunities during daily routines such as riding in the car, bedtime, doing laundry, putting away groceries, planning schedules, and so on.

Name _____

Position

Main Idea

I will use position words to tell where objects are.

Vocabulary

position

Position words tell where objects are.

above

far

behind
the bench

below
the flag

in front of
the bench

down
the slide

up
the
ladder

next
to

TICKETS

to the **left** of

to the **right** of

Use the position words to draw.

1.  in front of

2. left of

3. above

4. near

5. **Talk About It** Can an object have more than one position word that tells where it is? Give an example.

GO on

Name _____

Look at the picture. Circle the position word.

6.

The goes _____ the  .

up   down

7.

The  is to the _____ of the  .

left   right

8.

The  is _____ the .

behind   in front of

9.

The is _____ the  .

above   below

Problem Solving

Follow the directions.

10. In the middle of the page, draw a green △ in the middle of a ☐.

11. Draw a ☐ to the right of the ☐.

12. Draw a red △ above the ☐.

13. Draw a ○ on top of the red △.

Math at Home Activity: Choose an object and have your child guess what it is by answer position clues such as: It is above the television, it is behind the curtain.

Name _____

Make New Figures

Get Ready

Main Idea

I will use pattern blocks to make new figures.

You can make new figures by putting other figures together.

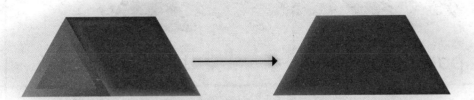

Check

Use pattern blocks to make a new figure. Draw the new figure.

Figure	Use	Draw your figure.
1.  hexagon	trapezoid	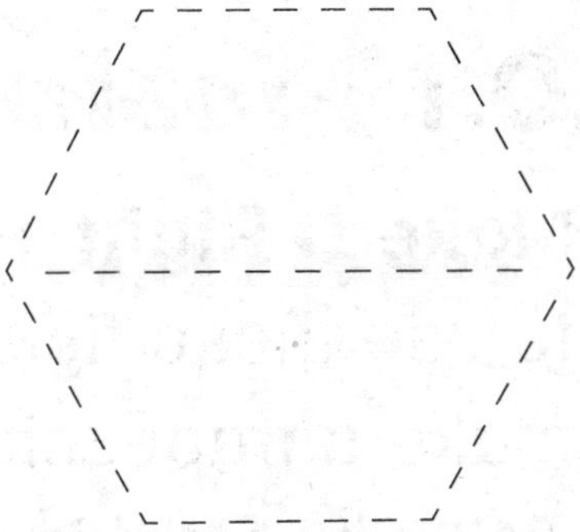
2. trapezoid	 triangle	

3. **Talk About It** How can you find out which figures are needed to make a new figure?

Use pattern blocks to make a new figure.
Draw the new figure.

Figure	Use	Draw your figure.
4. parallelogram	triangle	
5. hexagon	parallelogram triangle trapezoid	

H.O.T. Problem

6. Make It Right Paul tried to use these figures to make a trapezoid. Tell why Paul is wrong. Make it right. Draw the missing figure.

_ _

_ _

_ _

Math at Home Activity: Go on a shape scavenger hunt! While driving or walking, draw attention to doors and windows in the shape of rectangles, road signs in the shape of triangles, and roofs in the shape of trapezoids.

Name _____

Give and Follow Directions

Main Idea

I will give and follow directions.

You can use a grid to show direction.

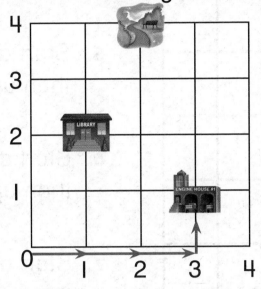

Start at 0.
Go right 3,
up 1.

Where
are you?

I am at the
fire house!

Check

Follow the directions. Circle where you are.

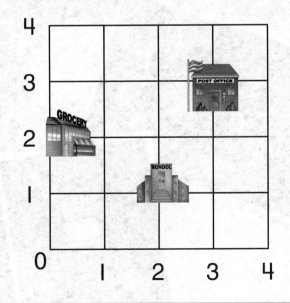

1. Start at 0. Go right 3, then up 3.

2. Start at 0. Go up 2.

3.  How could you go from the school
to the post office?

Follow the directions. Draw the object.

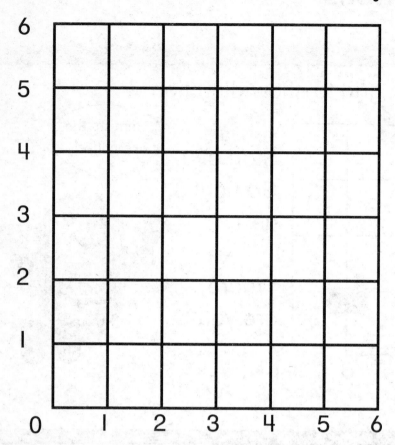

4. Start at 0. Go right 1, then up 4. Draw a 🏠.

5. Start at 0. Go right 6, then up 1. Draw a 🚚.

6. Start at 0. Go right 3, then up 2. Draw a 🌳 .

7. Start at 0. Go right 6, then up 6. Draw a ☀.

Data File

This is the state flag of Pennsylvania. The flag is red, white, and blue.

8. What shape is the flag?

    rectangle   circle

9. The bird is _____ the boat.

    below   above

Math at Home Activity: Draw another object on the grid above. Have your child give directions on how to get to that object from the house.

Rosie made a picture of flowers.

Circle the rectangles.

FOLD DOWN

Real-World MATH

Shapes can be used to make art.

This book belongs to

_____

Problem Solving
in Art

Alyssa is using crayons to make a picture of her classroom. She needs 18 squares in her picture to show the students' desks. How many more squares does she need to draw?

—— squares

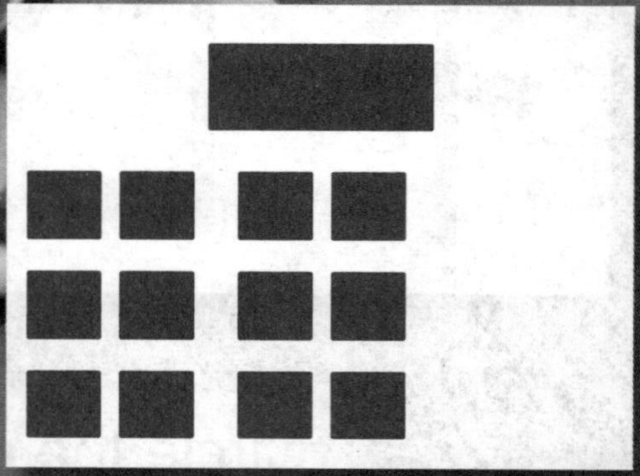

Steve is painting a picture.

How many circles can you find?

—— circles

Name _____

Vocabulary

Match the picture to the word.

1. pyramid

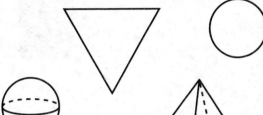

4. cone

2. square

5. triangle

3. sphere

6. circle

Concepts

Look at the three-dimensional figure.
Circle the objects with the same shape.

7.

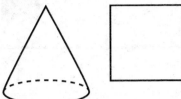

cone

Write how many.

8.

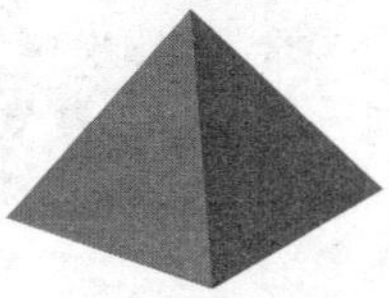

9.

10.

_____ corners

_____ corners

_____ corners

_____ faces

_____ faces

_____ faces

Look at the three-dimensional figure.
Circle the shape of the face.

11.   ☐

12. △

Circle the answer.

13. I have 2 faces and 0 corners.
Each face is a circle.
What am I?

Follow the directions. Circle where you are.

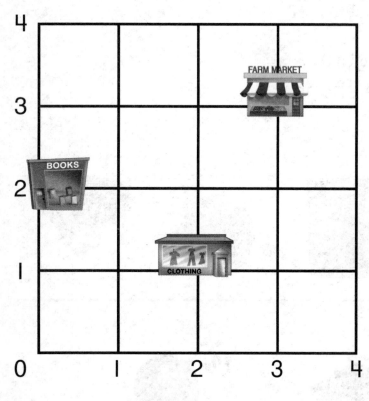

14. Start at 0. Go up 2.

15. Start at 0. Go right 3,
then up 3.

16. Start at 0. Go up 1,
then right 2.

Problem Solving

17. Use the grid above. Start at 0.
Draw a tree at right 4, up 4.

Summative Assessment

Name _____

Listen as your teacher reads each problem.
Choose the correct answer.

1.

⬭   ⬭

⬭   ⬭

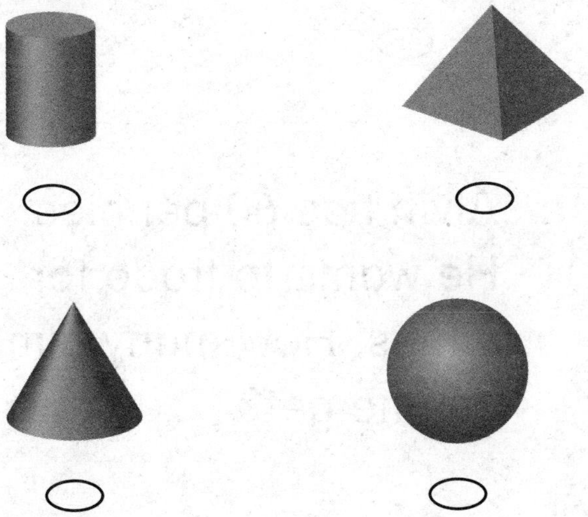

4.
[ ]

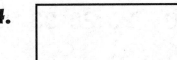
⬭   ⬭

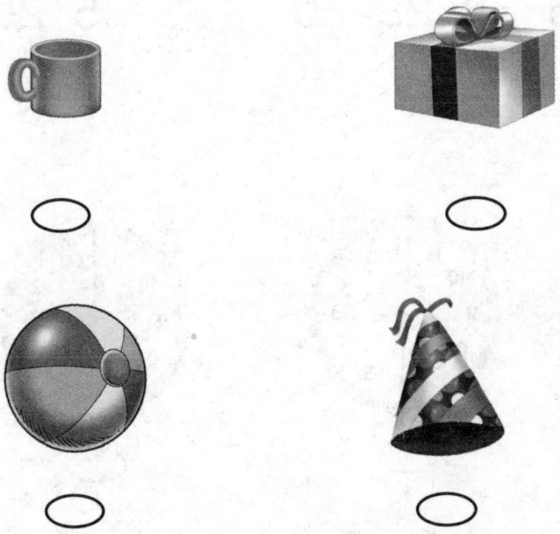

⬭   ⬭

2. 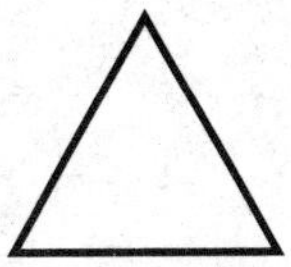
△

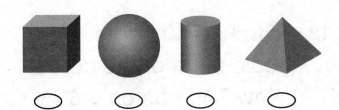
⬭   ⬭   ⬭   ⬭

5.
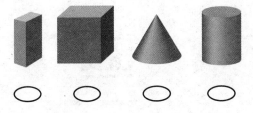
⬭   ⬭   ⬭   ⬭

3.
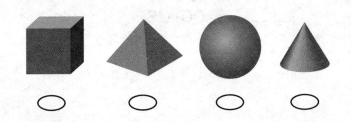
⬭   ⬭   ⬭   ⬭

6.

25¢   30¢   35¢   45¢
⬭   ⬭   ⬭   ⬭

four hundred thirteen   **413**

7.

| 20 | 45 | 33 | 28 |

28 45 33 20   20 28 33 45
◯   ◯

45 33 28 20   33 45 20 28
◯   ◯

8.

◯

◯

◯

◯

9.

◯   ◯   ◯   ◯

10.

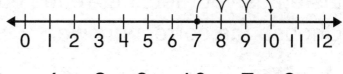

0 1 2 3 4 5 6 7 8 9 10 11 12

6 + 3 = 9   10 − 7 = 3
◯   ◯

7 + 3 = 10   3 + 4 = 7
◯   ◯

11. Alvin has 60 pennies.
He wants to trade for
dimes. How many dimes
can he get?

_____ dimes

12. Tito had 10 cards. Kela
took some of the cards.
Now Tito has only 6
cards. How many cards
did Kela take?

_____ cards

Summative Assessment

STOP

Understand Place Value

Key Vocabulary

tens

regroup

Explore

What house number is after 26 and before 28?

_____

Walter Bibikow/Index Stock Imagery

Math Online
Take the Chapter Readiness
Quiz at macmillanmh.com.

 Are You Ready for Chapter 13?

Circle to make groups of 10.

1.

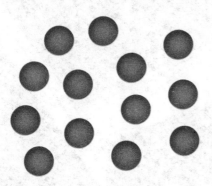

2.

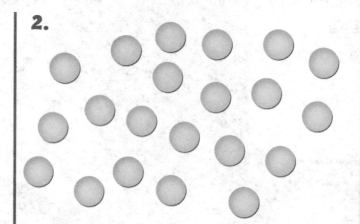

3. Say and write the missing numbers.

1	2	3		5	6	7	8	9	
11		13	14	15		17	18	19	20
21	22	23		25	26	27	28		30

Circle groups of 10. Count. Write the number.

4.

_____ frogs

5. There are 4 boxes on the floor.
Each box has 10 red balls in it.
How many balls in all?

_____ balls

This page checks skills needed for Chapter 13.

MATH at HOME

Dear Family,

Today my class started Chapter 13, **Understand Place Value**. In this chapter, I will learn to count, read, write, and compare numbers to 100. Here is an activity we can do and a list of books we can read together.

Love, _____

Activity

Write fifteen different numbers that are less than 100 on separate pieces of paper. Put the numbers in a sack. Both of you draw a number. Ask your child to tell who has the greater number.

Key Vocabulary

tens this number has 2 tens

‖ ⋮

regroup to take apart a number to write it in a new way

Math Online > Click on the eGlossary link at macmillanmh.com to find out more about these words. There are 13 languages.

Books to Read

Betcha!
by Stuart J. Murphy
HarperCollins Children's
Books, 1997.

100th Day Worries
by Margery Cuyler
Simon & Schuster
Books for Young
Readers, 2005.

Coyotes All Around
by Stuart J. Murphy
HarperCollins Children's
Books, 2003.

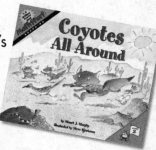

Estimada familia:

Hoy mi clase comenzó el Capítulo 13, **Comprende el valor de posición**. En este capítulo, aprenderé a contar, a leer, a escribir y a comparar números hasta 100. A continuación, hay una actividad que podemos hacer y una lista de libros que podemos leer juntos.

Cariños,

_____

Actividad

Escriban quince números diferentes menores de 100 en hojas de papel separadas. Coloquen los números en una bolsa. Saquen juntos un número. Pregúntenle a su hijo quién tiene el número menor.

Vocabulario clave

decenas este número tiene 2 decenas

‖ :

reagrupar reordenar los números en partes más simples

Math Online Visiten el enlace eGlossary en <u>macmillanmh.com</u> para averiguar más sobre estas palabras, las cuales se muestran en 13 idiomas.

Libros recomendados

Valor posicional
de Dinaielle Carroll
Yellow Umbrella Books, 2006.

Hacer decenas: grupos de gollyluvas
de John Burstein
Weekly Reader Early
Learning Library, 2006

Tens

Get Ready

Main Idea

I will count groups of ten.

Vocabulary

tens

 =

10 ones   1 ten

These cubes are in groups of 10. I can count by **tens** to find how many. 10, 20

Check

Use . Make groups of ten. Say and write the number.

1.

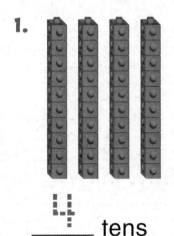

____ tens   40

Say: forty

2.

____ tens   ____

Say: seventy

Use . Make groups of ten. Say and write the number.

3.

_____ tens

_____

Say: twenty

4.

_____ tens

_____

Say: eighty

5.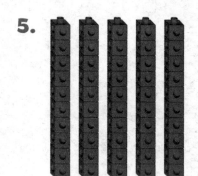

_____ tens

_____

Say: fifty

6.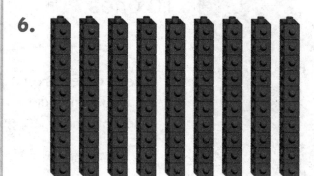

_____ tens

_____

Say: ninety

7.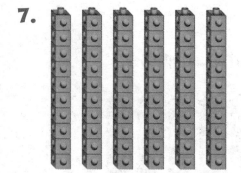

_____ tens

_____

Say: sixty

8.

_____ tens

_____

Say: thirty

9. **Talk About It** How would you use cubes to model the number 100?

GO on

Name _____

> **Practice**

Use . Make groups of ten. Say and write the number.

10.

Think: ten, twenty, thirty, forty.

_____ tens

_____

Say: forty

11.

_____ ten

_____

Say: ten

12.

_____ tens

_____

Say: twenty

13.

_____ tens

_____

Say: thirty

14.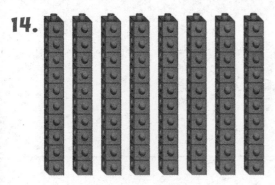

_____ tens

_____

Say: eighty

15.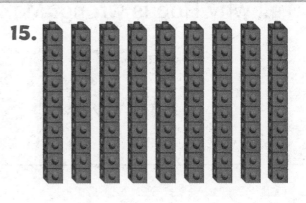

_____ tens

_____

Say: ninety

Use 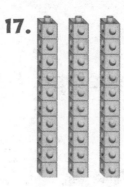. Make groups of ten. Say and write the number.

16.

_____ tens
_____
Say: one hundred

17.

_____ tens
_____
Say: thirty

18.

_____ tens
_____
Say: fifty

19.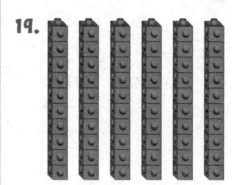

_____ tens
_____
Say: sixty

H.O.T. Problem

20. Make It Right Rob says there are 20 pennies.
Tell why Rob is wrong. Make it right.

_____

- -

_____

- -

_____

Math at Home Activity: Give your child several small items (buttons, pennies) to count. Help your child make groups of ten and then count by tens.

Name _____

Tens and Ones

Get Ready

Main Idea

I will make groups of tens and ones.

Vocabulary

regroup

You can show a number as tens and ones. You can **regroup** 10 ones as 1 ten.

Put together 10 ones to make 1 ten.

16 ones = 1 ten and 6 ones or 16

Check

Use . Make groups of tens and ones.
Write how many.

1.

14 ones = ___1___ ten and

___4___ ones   __14__

2.

18 ones = _____ ten and

_____ ones   _____

3. 21 ones = _____ tens and _____ one   _____

4. 52 ones = _____ tens and _____ ones   _____

5. **Talk About It** How would you regroup 20 ones?

Use 🎲. Make groups of tens and ones.
Write how many.

6.

13 ones = _____ ten and

_____ ones   _____

7.

26 ones = _____ tens and

_____ ones   _____

8.

17 ones = _____ ten and

_____ ones   _____

9. 35 ones = _____ tens and _____ ones   _____

10. 46 ones = _____ tens and _____ ones   _____

11. 67 ones = _____ tens and _____ ones   _____

12. 29 ones = _____ tens and _____ ones   _____

13. **WRITING IN ►MATH** Explain how to regroup
51 ones as tens and ones.

_____

_ _

_____

_ _

_____

Math at Home Activity: Ask your child to regroup 83 as
tens and ones.

Name _____

Count the objects in the picture.

1. How many trees are there? _____

   How many tens? _____

   How many ones? _____

2. How many dogs are there? _____

   How many tens? _____

   How many ones? _____

3. How many flowers are there? _____

   How many tens? _____

   How many ones? _____

4. How many dogs with red collars? _____

   How many tens? _____

   How many ones? _____

Lizzie the Lizard

Making Ten

Play with a partner. Take turns.

- Choose a 🎲. Place it on START.
- Roll the 🎲.
- Decide how many you would add to that number to make 10.
- Move that many foot prints.
- The first person to FINISH wins.

You Will Need

START

FINISH

Name _____

Problem-Solving Strategy
Guess and Check

Main Idea

I will guess and check to solve a problem.

Raj has 15 toy cars to put on 3 shelves. He wants to put the same number of cars on each shelf. How many cars go on each shelf?

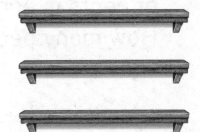

Understand

What do I know?
Underline what you know.
What do I need to find?
Circle the question.

Plan

How will I solve the problem?
I will use cubes to guess and check.

Solve

Put 4 cubes on each shelf.
Count the cubes. Only 12 cubes in all.
Try 5.

Check

Look back.
Is my answer reasonable?

Try It

Remember
Understand
Plan
Solve
Check

Guess and check to solve.

1. Brianna puts 12 pears into 2 bowls.
   She wants to put the same number
   of pears in each bowl.
   How many pears go in each bowl?

_____ pears

2. There are 3 stacks of pennies.
   There are 10 pennies in each stack.
   How many pennies are there in all?

_____ pennies

Your Turn

Guess and check to solve.

3. Ms. Kim has 18 balloons.
   She wants to give Rae and Doug
   the same number of balloons.
   How many balloons does she
   give each person?

_____ balloons

4. There are 4 spelling bee teams.
   Each team is made up of 5 students
   How many students are there altogether?

_____ students

Math at Home Activity: Give your child 40, 50, or 60 pennies. Ask
your child to guess and check to figure out how many equal stacks can be
made.

Name _____

Numbers to 50

Get Ready

Main Idea

I will show numbers to 50 using tens and ones.

Speech bubble: 2 tens and 3 ones is 23

Speech bubble: 3 tens and 2 ones is 32

Check

Use  and ▯ and WorkMat 7.

Show groups of tens and ones.

Say and write the numbers.

1.

tens	ones

_____ ten   _____ ones

Say: thirteen _____

2.

tens	ones

_____ tens   _____ ones

Say: twenty-four _____

Use 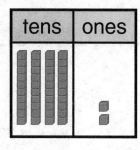 and ▪ and WorkMat 7.
Show groups of tens and ones.
Say and write the numbers.

3.

tens	ones

_____ tens

_____ ones

Say: forty-two _____

4.

tens	ones

_____ tens

_____ ones

Say: thirty-seven _____

5.

tens	ones

_____ tens

_____ one

Say: thirty-one _____

6.

tens	ones

_____ tens

_____ ones

Say: forty-eight _____

7.

tens	ones

_____ tens

_____ ones

Say: thirty-nine _____

8.

tens	ones

_____ tens

_____ ones

Say: twenty-six _____

9. How are 14 and 41 different?
How are they alike?

GO on

Name _____

Use 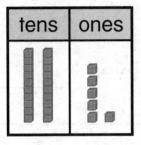 and ▪ and WorkMat 7.
Show groups of tens and ones.
Say and write the numbers.

10.

tens	ones

_____ tens

_____ ones

Say: twenty-six _____

11.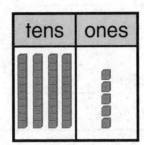

tens	ones

_____ tens

_____ ones

Say: forty-five _____

12.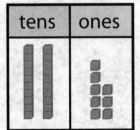

tens	ones

_____ tens

_____ ones

Say: twenty-eight _____

13.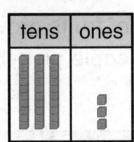

tens	ones

_____ tens

_____ ones

Say: thirty-three _____

14.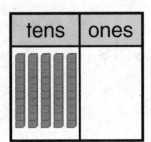

tens	ones

_____ tens

_____ ones

Say: fifty _____

15.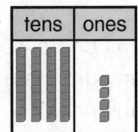

tens	ones

_____ tens

_____ ones

Say: forty-four _____

Use 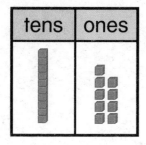 and ▪ and WorkMat 7. Show groups of tens and ones. Say and write the numbers.

16.

tens	ones

_____ tens

_____ ones

Say: nineteen _____

17.

tens	ones

_____ tens

_____ ones

Say: forty-seven _____

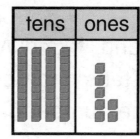

Data File

Many kinds of fruits grow on trees in Maryland. People pick the fruits and eat them.

Fruits Picked	
Fruit	**Number Picked**
Apples	31
Peaches	24
Pears	46
Plums	18

18. How many pears were picked? _____ pears

How many groups of ten? _____

How many ones? _____

19. How many peaches were picked?

_____

Stone+/Getty Images

Math at Home Activity: Put a number of objects (less than 50) out for your child. Have him or her place them in groups of tens and ones and say the number.

Name _____

Numbers to 100

Get Ready

Main Idea

I will write numbers in different ways.

You can write numbers in different ways.

tens	ones

tens	ones
4	2

_____ tens _____ ones

_____ Say: forty-two

Check

Use  and ▬ and WorkMat 7.
Show groups of tens and ones.
Write the number in different ways.

1.

tens	ones

tens	ones
3	1

_____ tens _____ one

31 Say: thirty-one

2.

tens	ones

tens	ones

_____ tens _____ ones

_____ Say: twenty-four

3. 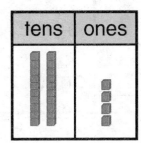 **Talk About It** How can you write 72 in more than one way?

Use  and ▪ and WorkMat 7.
Show groups of tens and ones.
Write the number in different ways.

4.

tens	ones
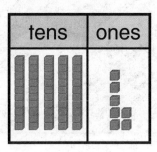	

_____ tens _____ ones

tens	ones

_____ Say: sixty-two

5.

tens	ones

_____ tens _____ ones

tens	ones

_____ Say: fifty-seven

6.

tens	ones
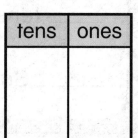	

_____ tens _____ ones

tens	ones

_____ Say: eighty-five

7.

tens	ones
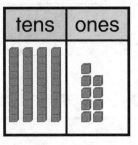	

_____ tens _____ ones

tens	ones

_____ Say: forty-nine

Practice with Technology

Model Place Value • Computer

Use place value mat to make numbers.
Choose a mat to show place value.

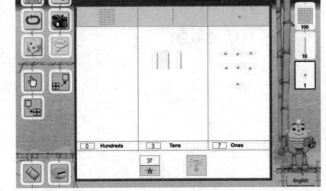

Stamp out 3 ▬▬▬▬▬

Stamp out 7 ▪

What is the number? **37**

---

8. You can use the computer to stamp out tens and ones.
Then write the number.

Stamp Out		Write the number.
▮	▪	
9	3	**93**
7	8	
8	0	
5	3	
4	4	
6	6	

9. Stamp out ▬▬▬ and ▪ to make each number. Complete the chart.

Use the computer to model each number.

Write the number.	Stamp Out	
	 ▮ (ten)	▪ (one)
89	8	9
71		1
43		
59		9
11		
62		
58	5	

Problem Solving

10. Number Sense Explain how to show 84 with only 7 tens.

_____

_____

_____

_____

Math at Home Activity: Ask your child to show 64 in at least two different ways.

Name _____

Count groups of ten. Write the number.

1. 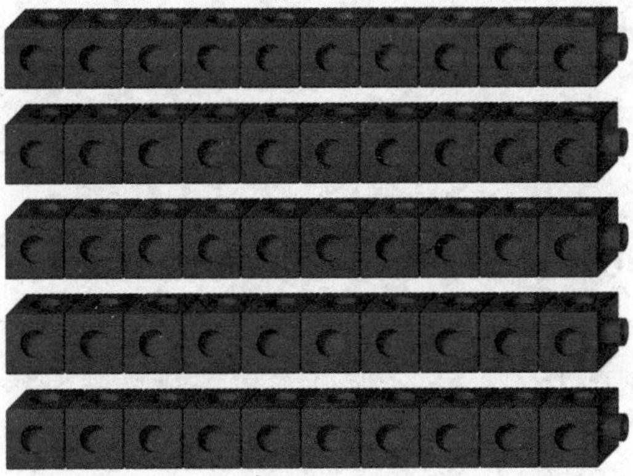 _____ tens

    _____ fifty

2.  _____ tens

    _____ thirty

Write the number.

3. 56 ones = _____ tens and _____ ones _____

4. 23 ones = _____ tens and _____ ones _____

Write the number in different ways.

5.
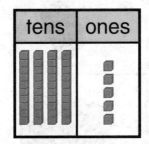

tens	ones

_____ tens _____ ones

_____

6. 4 boys each have 4 toy trains.
    How many trains do they have in all?

    _____

7. Libby wanted to measure her math book.

First she used  to measure.

Then she used 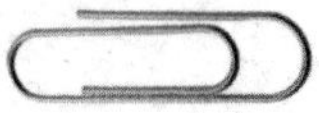 to measure.

Did she use fewer  or ?

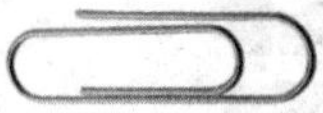

_____

Write number sentences to show fact families.

8. 7 + 6 = _____

_____ ◯ _____ = _____

_____ ◯ _____ = _____

_____ ◯ _____ = _____

9. 3 + 9 = _____

_____ ◯ _____ = _____

_____ ◯ _____ = _____

_____ ◯ _____ = _____

Look at the two-dimensional figure.
Circle the objects that have a face that shape.

10.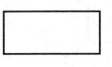

11.

12.

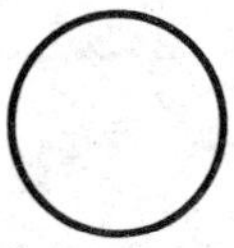

Formative Assessment

Name _____

Estimate Numbers

Main Idea

I will estimate numbers.

Review Vocabulary

estimate

You can estimate to find out *about* how many.

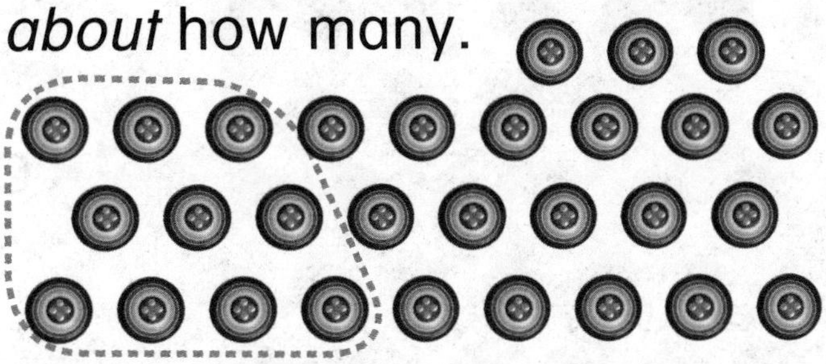

About how many buttons are there?

Estimate: _30_   Count: _29_

Circle 10. Estimate. Then count to find the exact number.

Check

Circle 10. Estimate about how many. Then count.

1.

Estimate: _50_

Count: _52_

2.

Estimate: _____

Count: _____

3. **Talk About It** How does circling 10 help you estimate?

Circle 10. Estimate about how many. Then count.

4.

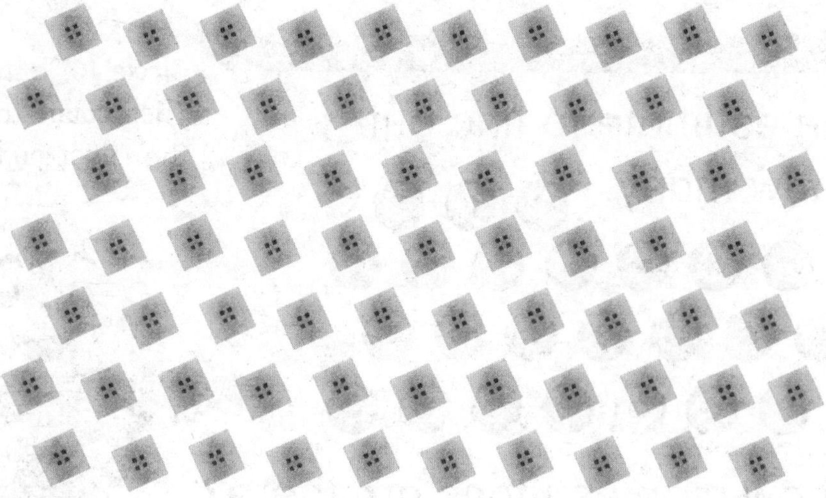

Estimate: _____

Count: _____

5.

Estimate: _____

Count: _____

6.

Estimate: _____

Count: _____

Problem Solving

7. Number Sense Natalie estimates that she has about 70 flowers. Which number shows how many flowers she could have?

12   53   72   100

Math at Home Activity: Give your child a handful of dry cereal or dry pasta. Ask your child to estimate how many. Then have him or her count to find the exact amount.

Problem-Solving Investigation

Main Idea

I will choose a strategy to solve a problem.

Your Mission:
Find the groups of 10 and how many more.

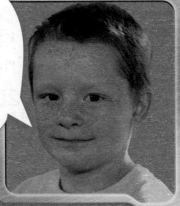

I have 23 cubes. I put them in groups of 10. How many groups of 10 do I have? How many more?

Understand

What do I know?
Underline what you know.
What do I need to find?
Circle it.

Plan

How will I solve the problem?
One way is to act it out.

Solve

Act it out.
I will use cubes to model the problem.

_____ groups of ten and _____ more

Check

Look back.
Is my answer reasonable?

Choose a strategy. Solve.

1. Mr. Kelley is counting beans
   to use during math.
   He needs 20 beans.
   How many groups of 10 will he have?

_____ groups of ten beans

2. Rita has 15 stickers to give
   to her 3 friends. How many stickers will
   each friend get?

_____ stickers

3. Jesse gets 10 grapes in a bag for lunch
   everyday. How many grapes does he
   get in total in 5 days?

_____ grapes

4. At Bob's Market there are 8 packages of
   baseball cards. Dustin wants to buy all of
   them. Each package costs 10¢. He also
   wants to buy a marble that costs 3¢.
   How much money will Dustin need?

_____ ¢

Math at Home Activity: Take advantage of problem-solving
opportunties during daily routines such as riding in the car, bedtime, doing
laundry, putting away the groceries, planning schedules, and so on.

Name _____

Compare Numbers to 100

Get Ready

Main Idea

I will compare two numbers.

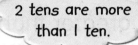
2 tens are more than 1 ten.

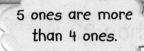
5 ones are more than 4 ones.

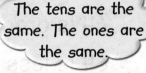
The tens are the same. The ones are the same.

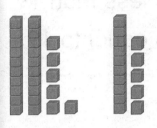
26 > 15
is greater than

34 < 35
is less than

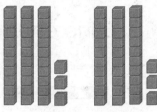
33 = 33
is equal to

Check

Use ▭▭▭▭ and ◼. Circle **is greater than**, **is less than**, or **is equal to**.

1. 17 (<) 31

   17 is greater than 31

   17 is less than 31

   17 is equal to 31

2. 36 (=) 36

   36 is greater than 36

   36 is less than 36

   36 is equal to 36

Use ▭▭▭▭ and ◼.
Write >, <, or =.

3. 27 ◯ 15

4. 99 ◯ 99

5. 47 ◯ 74

6. 60 ◯ 59

7. 63 ◯ 36

8. 51 ◯ 48

9. **Talk About It** How do you know 48 is greater than 38?

Practice

Use ▭▭▭ and ▪. Circle **is greater than**, **is less than**, or **is equal to**.

10. 64 (>) 23

     64 is greater than 23

     64 is less than 23

     64 is equal to 23

11. 19 (=) 19

     19 is greater than 19

     19 is less than 19

     19 is equal to 19

Use ▭▭▭ and ▪.
Write >, <, or =.

12. 41 ◯ 91

13. 53 ◯ 53

14. 87 ◯ 78

15. 37 ◯ 50

16. 56 ◯ 63

17. 99 ◯ 90

18. 82 ◯ 86

19. 45 ◯ 33

20. 92 ◯ 29

21. 49 ◯ 49

22. 70 ◯ 69

23. 68 ◯ 71

24. 84 ◯ 48

25. 63 ◯ 28

26. 10 ◯ 90

Problem Solving

27. Critical Thinking I have fewer than 25 acorns. I have more than 21 acorns. Draw how many acorns I could have.

Math at Home Activity: Write a number. Have your child name two numbers that are less than the number and two numbers that are greater. Ask your child what number is equal to the number.

Name _____

Order Numbers to 100

Main Idea

I will order numbers to 100.

Use a number line to order numbers.

85 is just **before** 86.
86 is **between** 85 and 87.
87 is just **after** 86.

80 81 82 83 84 85 86 87 88 89 90

Check

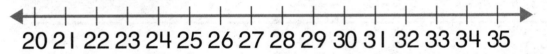

20 21 22 23 24 25 26 27 28 29 30 31 32 33 34 35

Write the number that is just **before**.

1. __27__ , 28   2. _____, 32   3. _____, 25

Write the number that is just **after**.

4. 20, _____   5. 33, _____   6. 23, _____

Write the number that is **between**.

7. 33, _____, 35   8. 21, _____, 23   9. 29, _____, 31

10. **Talk About It** How do you know what number comes just after 88?

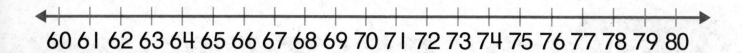

60 61 62 63 64 65 66 67 68 69 70 71 72 73 74 75 76 77 78 79 80

Write the number that is just **before**.

11. _____, 61   **12.** _____, 79   **13.** _____, 62

14. _____, 68   **15.** _____, 65   **16.** _____, 74

Write the number that is just **after**.

17. 63, _____   **18.** 71, _____   **19.** 66, _____

20. 73, _____   **21.** 60, _____   **22.** 69, _____

Write the number that is **between**.

23. 63, _____, 65   **24.** 71, _____, 73   **25.** 67, _____, 69

Problem Solving

26. Number Sense Rico has more than
34 pennies but fewer than 36 pennies.
How many pennies does he have? _____ pennies

27. Lydia found 1 penny.
Now she has 56 pennies.
How many pennies did she have before? _____ pennies

Math at Home Activity: Write two numbers on a piece of paper. Have your child tell you the numbers that come before, after, and between these numbers.

Steam is water as a gas.
This water is about 100 degrees.

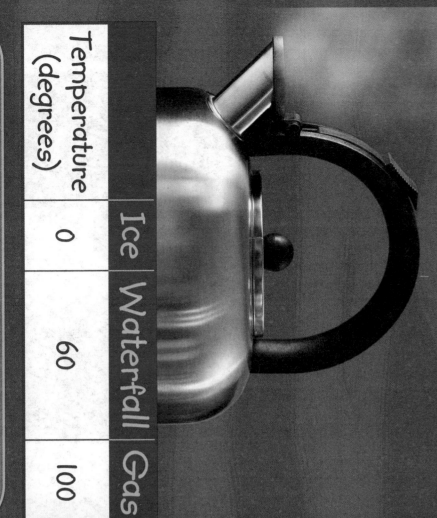

Temperature (degrees)	Ice	Waterfall	Gas
	0	60	100

Compare the temperatures. Use > and <.

0 degrees _____ 60 degrees

100 degrees _____ 0 degrees

Problem-Solving in Science

Real-World MATH

There is a lot of water on Earth.
Water can change.

This book belongs to

_____

_____

When water gets cold, it turns to ice. Ice is water as a solid.

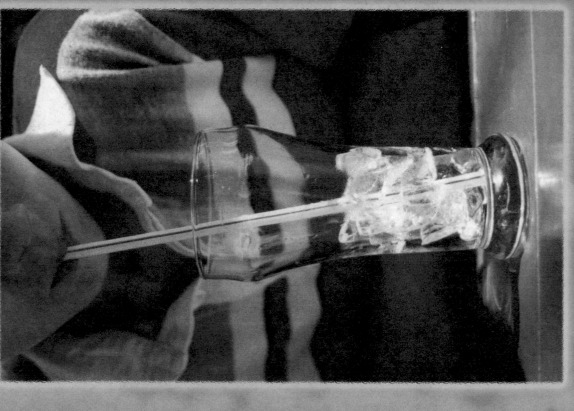

This water is about 0 degrees.

C

This is liquid water. It is like the water in your bathtub.

This water is about 60 degrees.

B

Name _____

Vocabulary

Draw lines to match.

1. regroup

2. tens

a. a group of 10 ones

b. to group numbers into tens and ones

Concepts

Count groups of ten. Write the number.

3.

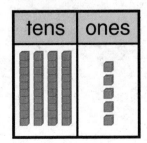

_____ tens _____ ones _____ Say: twenty

Write the number.

4. 75 ones = _____ tens and _____ ones _____

5. 92 ones = _____ tens and _____ ones _____

Write the number in different ways.

6.

tens	ones

_____ tens _____ ones

tens	ones

_____

Circle groups of ten. Write the number.

7.

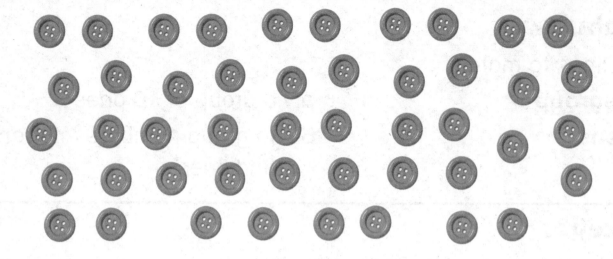

_____ tens   _____ ones   _____

Write the sign. Use > or <.

8. 41 ◯ 91   9. 37 ◯ 50   10. 86 ◯ 82

Write the number that is just **after**.

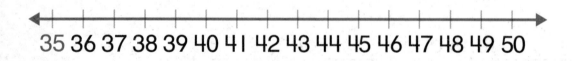

35 36 37 38 39 40 41 42 43 44 45 46 47 48 49 50

11. 37, _____   12. 39, _____   13. 41, _____

14. 35, _____   15. 49, _____   16. 45, _____

Problem Solving

17. Sue had 25 beads. She ties 5
beads on every piece of string.
How many pieces of string
does she need? ____ pieces

Summative Assessment

Name _____

Listen as your teacher reads each problem.
Choose the correct answer.

1.

16   20   60   100
○   ○   ○   ○

4.

1 ten	2 tens
3 ones	2 ones
○	○

2 tens	3 tens
3 ones	2 ones
○	○

2. 56   5 tens   4 tens
                 6 ones   8 ones
                   ○   ○

                 6 tens   5 tens
                 5 ones   3 ones
                   ○   ○

5.

10   20   30   40
○   ○   ○   ○

3.

tens	ones
7	2

27   62   67   72
○   ○   ○   ○

6.

○   ○   ○   ○

7.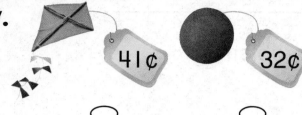

 41¢   ⚫ 32¢

◯   ◯

 55¢   60¢

◯   ◯

10.

$$10 - 3 \bigcirc 7$$

−   +
◯   ◯

>   =
◯   ◯

8.

$$4 + 3 = 7 \qquad 6 + 6 = 12$$
◯   ◯

$$7 + 7 = 14 \qquad 8 + 8 = 16$$
◯   ◯

11. The puppet show starts at 3:30. If it is an hour long, what time is it over?

_____

9.

$$5, 10, 15, 20, 25, 30$$

35   55
◯   ◯

50   40
◯   ◯

12. The hour hand points to 7. The minute hand points to 12. What time is it?

_____

Summative Assessment

Describe Fractional Parts

Key Vocabulary
equal parts
fraction
one half
one third
one fourth

Explore
Hillary cut the pizza into equal parts. How many equal parts are there? _____

Name _____

Math Online
Take the Chapter Readiness
Quiz at macmillanmh.com.

Are You Ready for Chapter 2?

1. Circle the shape that is divided into 2 equal parts.

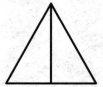

2. Circle the shape that is divided into 4 equal parts.

 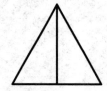 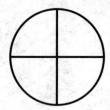

3. Color 1 out of 4 shamrocks green.

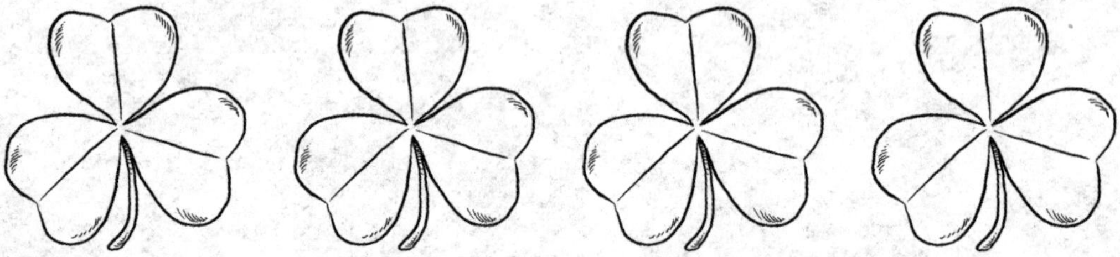

4. Marcia has these crayons. How many
out of the 8 crayons are blue?

_____ crayons

This page checks skills needed for Chapter 14.

MATH at HOME

Dear Family,

Today my class started Chapter 14, **Describe Fractional Parts**. In this chapter, I will learn how to name equal parts of a whole. Here is an activity we can do and a list of books we can read together.

Love, _____

Activity

Have your child practice naming equal parts of a whole in everyday situations. For example, show your child how to cut a sandwich in halves and then in fourths.

Key Vocabulary

equal parts each part is the same size

one half a fraction that shows 1 part out of 2 equal parts

Math Online Click on the eGlossary link at macmillanmh.com to find out more about these words. There are 13 languages.

Books to Read

Fraction Action
by Loreen Leedy
Holiday House, 1996.

Apple Fractions
by Jerry Pallotta
Cartwheel,
2003.

Fraction Fun
by David A. Adler
Holiday House,
1997.

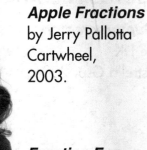

Estimada familia,

Hoy mi clase comenzó el Capítulo 14, **Describe partes fraccionarias.** En este capítulo, aprenderé a nombrar partes iguales de un todo. A continuación, hay una actividad que podemos hacer y una lista de libros que podemos leer juntos.

Cariños, _____

Actividad

Pídanle a su hijo(a) que practique nombrando partes iguales de un todo en situaciones cotidianas. Por ejemplo, muéstrenle a su hijo(a) cómo cortar un sándwich en mitades y luego en cuartos.

Vocabulario clave

partes iguales cada parte tiene el mismo tamaño

una mitad una fracción que muestra 1 parte de 2 partes iguales

Math Online > Visiten el enlace eGlossary en macmillanmh.com para averiguar más sobre estas palabras, las cuales se muestran en 13 idiomas.

Libros recomendados

Sumar y restar
de DK
Estrella Gsp, 2006.

Uno, dos, tres el año se fue
de Gregory Tang
Everest Publishing, 2004.

Hands-On Activity

Equal Parts

Copyright © Macmillan/McGraw-Hill, a division of The McGraw-Hill Companies, Inc.

Get Ready

Main Idea

I will identify equal parts.

Vocabulary

equal parts

Equal parts make a whole.

This shape has 4 equal parts. The parts are all the same shape and same size.

Check

Place pattern blocks on the matching shapes.
Write how many equal parts.

1.

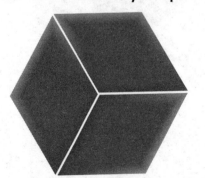

_____ equal parts

2.

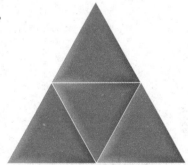

_____ equal parts

3.

_____ equal parts

4. Talk About It   How do you know the parts are equal?

Circle the picture that shows equal parts.

5.

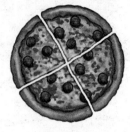  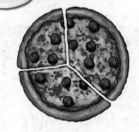

6.

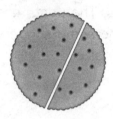 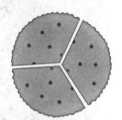 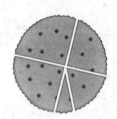

Draw a line or lines to show equal parts.

7.

2 equal parts

8.

3 equal parts

9.

4 equal parts

10.

4 equal parts

Problem Solving

11. Visual Thinking Samantha cut this sandwich to share. How many children are going to eat the sandwich?

_____ children

Name _____

Problem-Solving Strategy
Draw a Picture

Main Idea

I will draw a picture to solve a problem.

Jo made a sandwich. She wants to share the sandwich with her sister and her brother. Jo needs to cut her sandwich into equal parts. How many equal parts?

Understand

What do I know?

Underline what you know.

What do I need to find?

Circle the question.

Plan

How will I solve the problem?

Solve

Draw a picture.

Draw a square.

Make equal parts for Jo, her sister, and her brother.

Count the equal parts.

_____ equal parts

Check

Look back.

Is my answer reasonable?

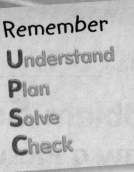

Try It

Draw a picture to solve.

1. Liz and Koto want to draw pictures for their teacher. There is only one piece of paper left. They need to share the piece of paper equally. How many parts do they need?

_____equal parts

2. Jeff is making the same bracelets for three of his friends. He has one long piece of yarn. How many equal pieces of yarn does he need?

_____equal pieces

Your Turn

Draw a picture to solve.

3. Carlos wants to share his orange equally with his friend. How many parts does he need?

_____equal parts

4. Grant is sharing a small pizza equally with 3 of his cousins. How many parts does Grant need?

_____equal parts

Math at Home Activity: Have your child gather objects in your home to write a guess and check problem for you to solve together.

Name _____

One Half

Get Ready

Main Idea

I will name equal parts of a whole.

Vocabulary

fraction

one half

You can use a **fraction** to tell about equal parts.

One half of the pie is shaded.

I out of 2 total parts is $\frac{1}{2}$ of the pie.

Check

Choose a . Color one half.

1.

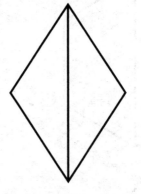

2.

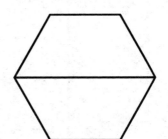

3.

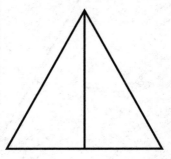

4.

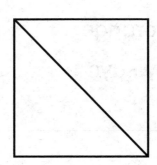

5.

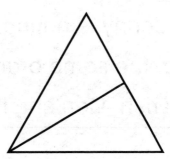

6.

7. **Talk About It** How could you share a sandwich with your friend?

Choose a . Color one half.

8.

9.

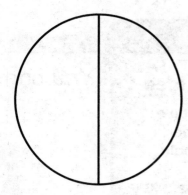

10.

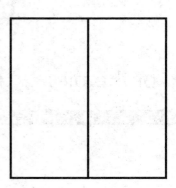

11.

12.

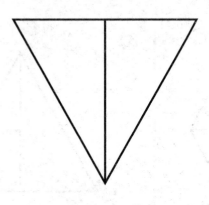

13.

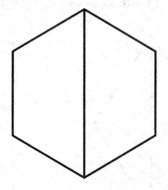

Problem Solving

14. **Critical Thinking** Jenny is eating $\frac{1}{2}$ of an orange. Trish is eating $\frac{1}{2}$ of the same orange. Jenny says she has less than Trish. Can she be right?

_____

_ _ _ _ _ _ _ _ _ _ _ _ _ _ _ _

_____

_ _ _ _ _ _ _ _ _ _ _ _ _ _ _ _

_____

462   four hundred sixty-two

One Third and One Fourth

Get Ready

Main Idea

I will name parts of a whole.

Vocabulary

one third

one fourth

One third and **one fourth** are fractions that name parts of a whole.

Thirds

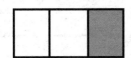

I out of 3 total parts is blue. $\frac{1}{3}$ is blue.

Fourths

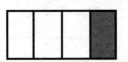

I out of 4 total parts is red. $\frac{1}{4}$ is red.

Check

The top number is the number of colored parts. The bottom number is the number of parts in all.

Write the fraction.

1. 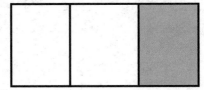 $\frac{1}{3}$

2. 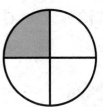   _____

Color I equal part. Circle the fraction. Fill in the numbers.

3.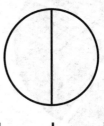

$\frac{1}{2}$ $\frac{1}{3}$ $\frac{1}{4}$

___ out of ___ parts

4.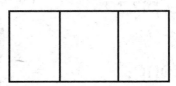

$\frac{1}{2}$ $\frac{1}{3}$ $\frac{1}{4}$

___ out of ___ parts

5.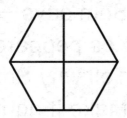

$\frac{1}{2}$ $\frac{1}{3}$ $\frac{1}{4}$

___ out of ___ parts

6. **Talk About It** How are $\frac{1}{3}$ and $\frac{1}{4}$ different?

Write the fraction for the piece that was eaten.

7.

8.

_____   _____

Color 1 equal part. Circle the fraction. Fill in the numbers.

9.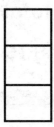

$\frac{1}{2}$ $\frac{1}{3}$ $\frac{1}{4}$

___ out of ___ parts

10.

$\frac{1}{2}$ $\frac{1}{3}$ $\frac{1}{4}$

___ out of ___ parts

11.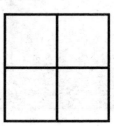

$\frac{1}{2}$ $\frac{1}{3}$ $\frac{1}{4}$

___ out of ___ parts

H.O.T. Problem

12. Make It Right

Sam says $\frac{1}{3}$ of the pizza has pepperoni.
Tell why Sam is wrong.
Make it right.

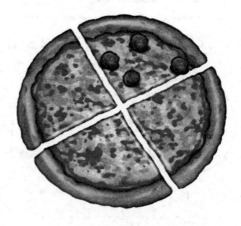

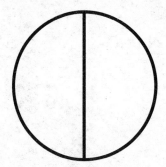

Name _____

Use 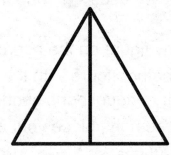. Shade $\frac{1}{2}$ or 1 of the 2 parts.

1.

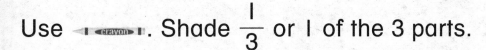

2.

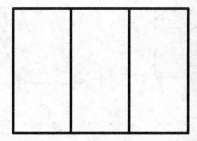

Use 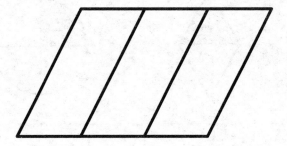. Shade $\frac{1}{3}$ or 1 of the 3 parts.

3.

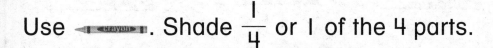

4.

Use 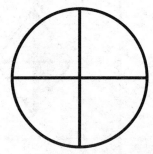. Shade $\frac{1}{4}$ or 1 of the 4 parts.

5.

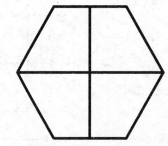

6.

The Equalizer
Fractions

Play with a partner. Take turns.
- One player uses  and the other uses .
- Pick any figure on the board.
- Find another figure with the same number of equal parts shaded.
- If you are right, place your counters on both spaces.
- The person with the most counters on the board wins.

You Will Need

 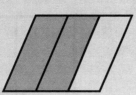 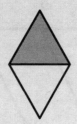 

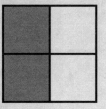 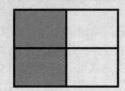 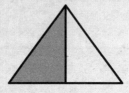 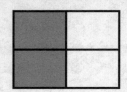

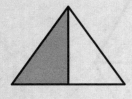 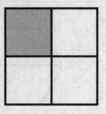 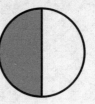 

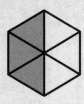 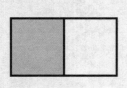 

Name _____

Write how many equal parts.

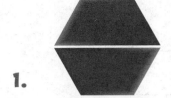

1. _____ equal parts

2. _____ equal parts

3. _____ equal parts

Use . Shade one half.

4.

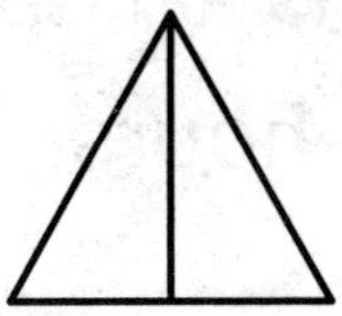

5.

Use . Shade 1 of the 3 parts.

6.

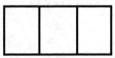

7.

Use . Shade $\frac{1}{4}$.

8.

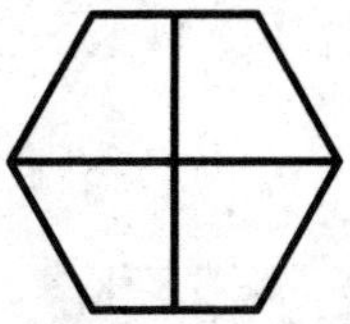

9.

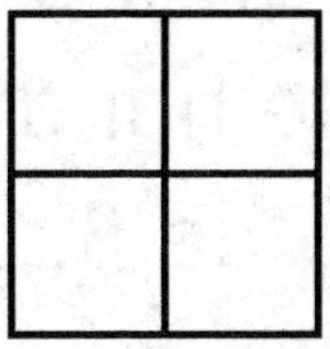

Write the numbers.

10. 99 ones = _____ tens _____ ones   _____

11. 12 ones = _____ ten _____ ones   _____

12. 53 ones = _____ tens _____ ones   _____

---

13. Circle the event that takes the most time.

I hour   half hour   2 hours

---

14. Rosa has 4 pencils. She bought 9 more. How many pencils does she have now?

_____ ◯ _____ ◯ _____

15. Darin has 11 shirts. He gave 5 to his brother. How many shirts does he have now?

_____ ◯ _____ ◯ _____

---

16. Solve the riddle. Draw the hands on the clock. My minute hand is on the 12. My hour hand is on the 8.

What time am I? _____ o'clock

Formative Assessment

Name _____

Non-Unit Fractions

Main Idea

I will describe whole objects or sets using non-unit fractions.

Some fractions can also describe more than one equal part.

$\frac{2}{3}$ or 2 out of 3 parts are shaded.

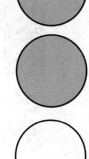

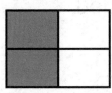

Check

Write how many parts are shaded.

1.

_____ out of _____ parts

2.

_____ out of _____ parts

Color to show each fraction.

3.

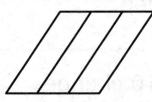

$\frac{2}{3}$ are shaded.

4.

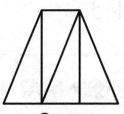

$\frac{3}{4}$ are shaded.

5. **Talk About It** If $\frac{3}{3}$ or 3 out of 3 parts are shaded, how much of the object would be shaded? Explain.

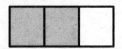
Write how many parts are shaded.

6.

_____ out of _____ parts

7.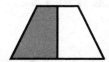

_____ out of _____ parts

8.

$\frac{3}{4}$ $\frac{1}{2}$ $\frac{1}{4}$

9.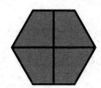

$\frac{2}{4}$ $\frac{1}{2}$ $\frac{4}{4}$

Color to show each fraction.

10.

$\frac{2}{4}$ are shaded.

11.

$\frac{3}{4}$ are shaded.

12.

$\frac{1}{3}$ is shaded.

13.

$\frac{1}{2}$ is shaded.

14. **WRITING IN ►MATH** How would Exercise 10 change

if $\frac{3}{4}$ was shaded instead of $\frac{2}{4}$?

_____

_____

_____

Name _____

Fractions of a Set

Get Ready

Main Idea

I will describe parts of a set.

You can use fractions to describe part of a set.

 _____ out of _____ leaves are yellow.

 _____ out of _____ leaves are orange.

 _____ out of _____ leaves are red.

✓ Check

Color to show each fraction.

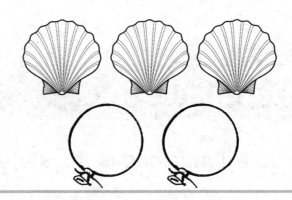

1. 2 out of 3 shells are yellow.

2. 1 out of 2 balloons are red.

Describe part of a set. Complete the sentence.

3.  _____ out of _____ cars are blue.

4. **Talk About It** If 3 out of 4 dogs are brown, how many dogs are brown? Explain.

Color to show each fraction.

5. 3 out of 7 sea stars are brown.

6. 2 out of 4 sea horses are green.

Describe part of a set. Complete the sentences.

7.

_____ out of _____ 🐙 are blue.

8.

_____ out of _____ 🐟 are yellow.

Data File

The Atlantic cod is the state fish of Massachusetts.

9. Describe part of the set.
_____ out of _____ fish are green.

Math at Home Activity: Collect 3 yellow crayons, 2 blue crayons, and 4 red crayons. Ask your child to tell you what fraction describes each color in the set of crayons.

Name _____

Problem-Solving Investigation

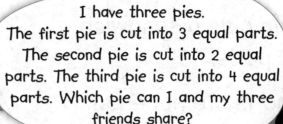

I have three pies.
The first pie is cut into 3 equal parts.
The second pie is cut into 2 equal
parts. The third pie is cut into 4 equal
parts. Which pie can I and my three
friends share?

Main Idea

I will choose a
strategy to
solve a
problem.

Your Mission:
Find out which pie Emma
and her friends can share.

Understand

What do I know? Underline what you know.
What do I need to find? Circle it.

Plan

How will I solve the problem?
One way is to guess and check.

Solve

Guess and check.

Can Emma and her friends share the first pie?

Can Emma and her friends share the second pie?

Can Emma and her friends share the third pie?

Check

Look back. Is my answer reasonable?

Try It

Choose a strategy. Solve.

1. Juanita cuts a sandwich into 2 parts.

   The parts are not equal.

   Circle Juanita's sandwich.

2. Eric is sharing a pie equally with 2 friends. How many pieces does he need?

   _____ equal pieces

Your Turn

Choose a strategy. Solve.

3. George and 2 friends share a pizza. Each boy eats 2 equal pieces.

   Circle the pizza they ate.

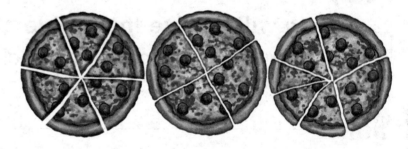

4. Theo makes 2 sandwiches. Sandwich 1 is cut into 2 equal parts. Sandwich 2 is cut into 3 equal parts. Which sandwich can Theo and his sister share equally?

   sandwich _____

Math at Home Activity: Take advantage of problem-solving opportunities during daily routines such as riding in the car, bedtime, doing laundry, putting away groceries, planning schedules, and so on.

D

Tracey picked these 10 tomatoes.

_____ out of _____ tomatoes are red.

FOLD DOWN

Problem Solving in Science

Real-World MATH

Many different things can grow in a garden. Two things that can grow are vegetables and flowers.

This book belongs to

_____

A

Jaden picked these 3 flowers. ___ out of ___ flowers are yellow.

Jorge picked these 6 peppers. ___ out of ___ peppers are green.

Name _____

Vocabulary

Draw lines to match.

1. **equal parts**   a. I out of 2 equal parts

2. **one half**   b. each part is the same size

3. **one fourth**   c. I out of 4 equal parts

4. **one third**   d. I out of 3 equal parts

Concepts

Circle how many parts are shaded.

5.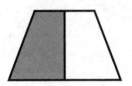

$\dfrac{1}{2}$ $\dfrac{1}{3}$ $\dfrac{1}{4}$

6.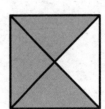

$\dfrac{1}{4}$ $\dfrac{2}{4}$ $\dfrac{3}{4}$

Show each fraction.

7.

$\dfrac{1}{3}$ is shaded

8.

$\dfrac{2}{2}$ are shaded

Describe part of a set. Complete the sentence below.

8.

_____ out of _____  is white.

9.

_____ out of _____  are red.

10.

_____ out of _____  are gold.

Problem Solving

11. Amos and Elton want a piece of chicken pot pie. Each of them wants an equal part. Draw lines to show how you would cut the pot pie.

Summative Assessment

Name _____

Listen as your teacher reads the problem.
Choose the best answer.

1.

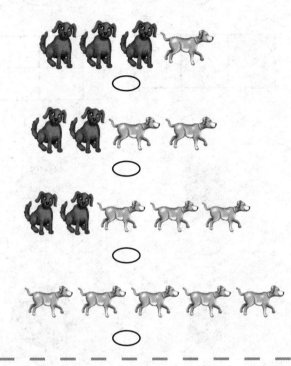

2.

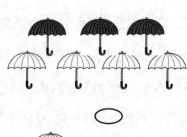

3.

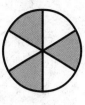

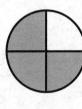

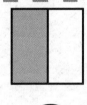
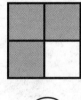
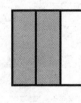

4.

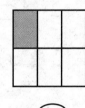

5.

◯ ◯

◯ ◯

6.

53¢ 48¢

◯ ◯

43¢ 33¢

◯ ◯

7.

◯ ◯

◯ ◯

8.

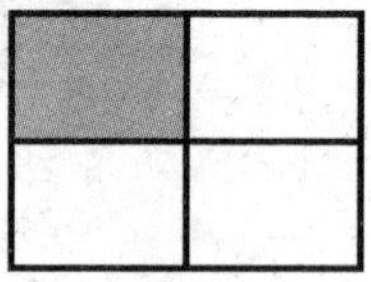

◯ ◯

◯ ◯

9.

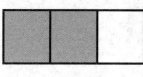

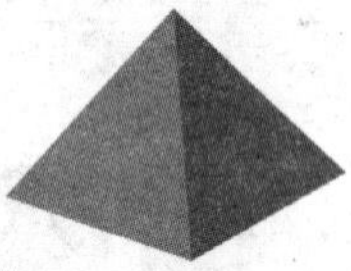

◯ ◯

◯ ◯

10. Tyrone had a sandwich he wanted to share with 2 friends. How many equal pieces should he cut it into?

_____ equal parts

11. Camille picked 9 flowers. 4 of the flowers were red, the rest were yellow. How many flowers were yellow?

_____ flowers

Summative Assessment

Solve Two-Digit Addition and Subtraction Problems

Key Vocabulary

round

Explore

What is 10 more than 14?

_____

What is 10 more than 18?

_____

Name _____

Are You Ready for Chapter 15?

Write how many tens and ones.

1.

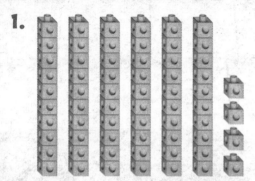

_____ tens _____ ones = _____

2.

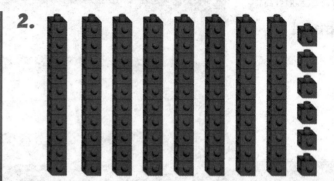

_____ tens _____ ones = _____

Add or subtract.

3. 9
     + 1

4. 15
     − 7

5. 4
     − 2

6. 12
     − 6

7. 9
     + 3

8. 4
     + 7

9. 14
     − 8

10. 8
     + 3

11. 7
     + 6

12. 13
     − 5

13. 10 more than 25 _____   **14.** 1 less than 50 _____

15. 1 more than 35 _____   **16.** 10 less than 60 _____

17. Maya counts 13 tadpoles. 5 of them swim away.
     How many tadpoles are left? _____ tadpoles

This page checks skills needed for Chapter 15.

MATH at HOME

Dear Family,

Today my class started Chapter 15, **Solve Two-Digit Addition and Subtraction Problems**. In this chapter, I will learn to add and subtract two-digit numbers. Here is an activity we can do and a list of books we can read together.

Love,

_____

Activity

Have your child practice adding and subtracting tens. For example, 4 dimes + 2 dimes = 6 dimes, 40¢ + 20¢ = 60¢.

Key Vocabulary

estimate to find a number close to an exact amount.

round to change the value of a number to one that is easier to work with.

Math Online > Click on the eGlossary link at macmillanmh.com to find out more about these words. There are 13 languages.

Books to Read

Arctic Fives Arrive
by Elinor J. Pinczes
Houghton Mifflin
Company, 1996.

The Cats of Mrs. Calamari
by John Stadler
Scholastic, Inc., 1997.

17 Kings and 42 Elephants
by Margaret Mahy
Dial, 1987.

Estimada familia:

Hoy mi clase comenzó el Capítulo 15, **Resuelva la adición del dos digito y problemas de sustracción**. En este capitulo, aprenderé a sumar y restar números de dos dígitos. A continuación, hay una actividad que podemos hacer y una lista de libros que podemos leer juntos.

Cariños,

Actividad

Pídanle a su hijo(a) que practique la suma y la resta de decenas. Por ejemplo, 4 monedas de 10¢ + 2 monedas de 10¢ = 6 monedas de 10¢, 40¢ + 20¢ = 60¢.

Vocabulario clave

estimar hallar un número cercano a la cantidad exacta

redondear cambiar el *valor* de un número a uno con el que es más fácil trabajar

Math Online Visiten el enlace eGlossary en macmillanmh.com para averiguar más sobre estas palabras, las cuales se muestran en 13 idiomas.

Libros recomendados

Sumar y restar
de DK
Estrella Gsp, 2006.

Una, dos, tres el año de fue
de Gregory Tang
Everest Publishing, 2004.

Name _____

Add and Subtract Tens

Get Ready

Main Idea

I will add and subtract tens.

Find 30 + 20.

3 tens + 2 tens = __5__ tens

30 + 20 = 50

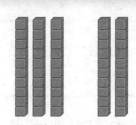

Find 50 − 10.

5 tens − 1 ten = __4__ tens

50 − 10 = 40

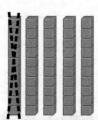

Check

Add or subtract. Use ▭▭▭▭ to help.

1. 4 tens + 2 tens = __6__ tens   40 + 20 = 60

2. 6 tens + 1 ten = _____ tens   60 + 10 = _____

3. 5 tens − 2 tens = _____ tens   50 − 20 = _____

4. 7 tens − 3 tens = _____ tens   70 − 30 = _____

5. **Talk About It** How does knowing 2 + 5 help you find 20 + 50?

Add or subtract. Use ▭▭▭▭▭▭ to help.

6. 2 tens + 6 tens = _____ tens   20 + 60 = _____

7. 6 tens + 3 tens = _____ tens   60 + 30 = _____

8. 5 tens + 4 tens = _____ tens   50 + 40 = _____

9. 8 tens + 1 ten = _____ tens   80 + 10 = _____

10. 6 tens − 3 tens = _____ tens   60 − 30 = _____

11. 8 tens − 6 tens = _____ tens   80 − 60 = _____

Data File

River Otters in North Carolina	
Day	**Number Seen**
Friday	10
Saturday	20
Sunday	30

12. How many more otters were seen on Sunday than on Friday? _____

13. How many otters were seen on Saturday and Sunday? _____

Math at Home Activity: Have your child tell you how many tens are in 40 + 20.

Name _____

Add with Two-Digit Numbers

Get Ready

Main Idea

I will add with two-digit numbers.

Find 25 + 2.

Step 1	**Step 2**	**Step 3**
Show each number.	Add the ones.	Add the tens.

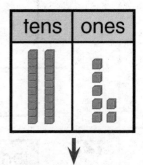

tens	ones
2	5
+	2

tens	ones
2	5
+	2
	7

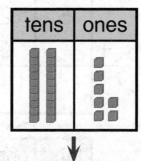

tens	ones
2	5
+	2
2	7

Add the ones.
2 ones + 5 ones
= 7 ones

The sum is
2 tens and
7 ones or 27.

Check

Use WorkMat 7 and  and ▪ . Add.

1.

tens	ones
1	3
+	4

2.

tens	ones
	6
+ 4	1

3.

tens	ones
	6
+ 5	3

4. Explain how you add tens and ones?

Use WorkMat 7 and ▭▭▭▭ and ▪ . Add.

> Remember start on the right.

5.

tens	ones
2	2
+	3

6.

tens	ones
4	2
+	2

7.

tens	ones
	4
+ 4	4

8.

tens	ones
5	2
+	6

9.

tens	ones
7	1
+	4

10.

tens	ones
	3
+ 9	1

11.

tens	ones
1	6
+	3

12.

tens	ones
5	5
+	4

13.

tens	ones
8	2
+	4

H.O.T. Problem

14. Make It Right

This is how Helen added 23 + 6. Tell why Helen is wrong. Make it right.

tens	ones
2	3
+ 6	
8	3

tens	ones
+	

_____

- -

_____

- -

_____

Copyright © Macmillan/McGraw-Hill, a division of The McGraw-Hill Companies, Inc.

Math at Home Activity: Your child learned to add a two-digit number and a one-digit number. Ask your child to explain how to add 42 + 5.

Problem-Solving Strategy
Guess and Check

Main Idea

I will guess and check to solve a problem.

Tara sees 2 colors of birds. She sees a total of 32 birds. Which 2 colors of birds did she see?

21   8   11

Understand

What do I know?
Underline what you know.
What do I need to find?
Circle the question.

Plan

How will I solve the problem?
I can guess and check.

Solve

Try 21 + 8 = 29   This is not correct.
    8 + 11 = 19   This is not correct.
  21 + 11 = 32   This is correct.
So Tara sees blue and yellow birds.

Check

Look back.
   Is my answer reasonable?

Try It

Use the guess and check strategy to solve.

1. Joan gets 2 colors of balloons. She gets 27 balloons in all.

13   14   11

What color balloons did she get? _____

2. Kim finds 2 colors of leaves. She finds 41 leaves in all.

20   16   21

What color leaves did she find? _____

Your Turn

Use the guess and check strategy to solve.

3. Rose bought 2 toys. She spent 17 cents altogether. What toys did she buy?

Rose bought a _____ and a _____.

4. Lena bought 2 toys. She spent 28 cents. What did she buy?

Lena bought a _____ and a _____.

Math at Home Activity: Give your child an addition or subtraction problem to solve using guess and check.

Add Two-Digit Numbers

Get Ready

Main Idea

I will add two-digit numbers.

Find 15 + 24.

Step 1
Show each number.

tens	ones
1	5
+ 2	4

Step 2
Add the ones.

tens	ones
1	5
+ 2	4
	9

Step 3
Add the tens.

tens	ones
1	5
+ 2	4
3	9

15 + 24 = 39

Check

Use WorkMat 7 and 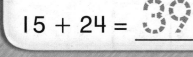 and ▪. Add.

1.

tens	ones
2	3
+ 1	4

2.

tens	ones
1	1
+ 3	6

3.

tens	ones
3	6
+ 1	3

4. **Talk About It** How did using addition facts help you?

Use WorkMat 7 and ▬▬▬▬ and ◼. Add.

5.

tens	ones
2	I
+ I	3

6.

tens	ones
4	2
+	2

7.

tens	ones
4	4
+ 2	4

8.

tens	ones
5	2
+ I	7

9.

tens	ones
6	2
+ I	4

10.

tens	ones
I	8
+ 6	I

11.

tens	ones
I	4
+ 2	3

12.

tens	ones
3	5
+ I	4

13.

tens	ones
8	2
+ I	4

Problem Solving

14. Reasoning The Bobcats score 12 points in the first half of the game. They score 21 points in the second half. How many points did they score in all?

_____

Math at Home Activity: Ask your child to explain how to find 81 + 4.

Name _____

Add.

1. 64¢ + 12¢ ____ ¢	**2.** 47¢ + 1¢ ____ ¢	**3.** 85¢ + 10¢ ____ ¢	**4.** 17¢ + 11¢ ____ ¢

5. 33¢ + 65¢ ____ ¢	**6.** 51¢ + 8¢ ____ ¢	**7.** 24¢ + 42¢ ____ ¢	**8.** 91¢ + 6¢ ____ ¢

9. 68¢ + 21¢ ____ ¢	**10.** 34¢ + 51¢ ____ ¢	**11.** 14¢ + 4¢ ____ ¢	**12.** 31¢ + 12¢ ____ ¢

13. 74¢ + 13¢ ____ ¢	**14.** 62¢ + 16¢ ____ ¢	**15.** 20¢ + 2¢ ____ ¢	**16.** 23¢ + 6¢ ____ ¢

Game Time

Adding Colors
Two-Digit Addition

You Will Need

Play with a partner. Take turns.

- Choose a ♟ and a color to start on.
- Spin the 🌀.
- Move to the color you spin by adding its number to the number you are on.
- If you are right, put a ⬤ down.
- The first person to cover all of the colors wins.

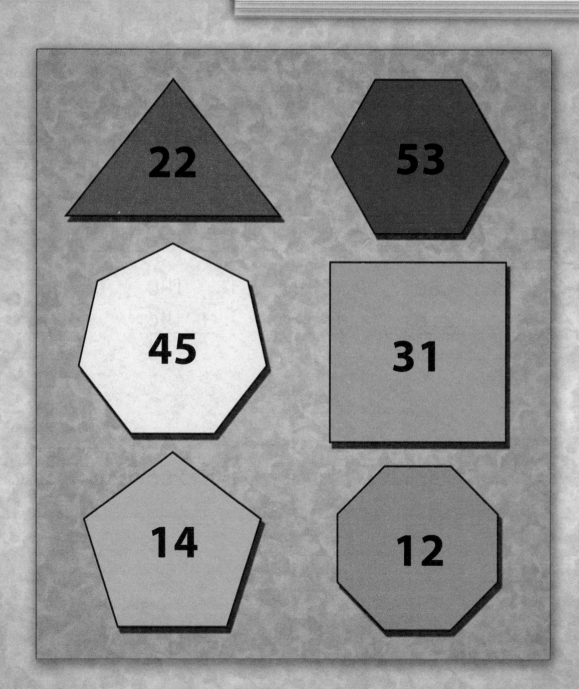

Name _____

Estimate Sums

Get Ready

Main Idea

I will estimate sums.

Vocabulary

round

Review Vocabulary

estimate

Sometimes when you add, you do not need an exact answer. You can estimate to find the sum.

Estimate 12 + 19.

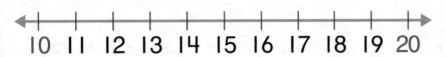

Step 1: Round to the nearest 10.

12 is closer to 10 ———▶ 12 rounds to 10.

19 is closer to 20 ———▶ 19 rounds to 20.

Step 2: Add.

10 + 20 = 30

> 1 + 2 = 3, so
> 10 + 20 = 30

Check

Round each number to the nearest ten. Then add.

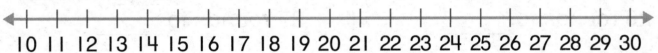

1. 17 + 21

   17 rounds to _____

   21 rounds to _____

   _____ + _____ = _____

2. 27 + 14

   27 rounds to _____

   14 rounds to _____

   _____ + _____ = _____

3. **Talk About It** Explain how you would estimate 33 + 31.

Round each number to the nearest ten. Then add.

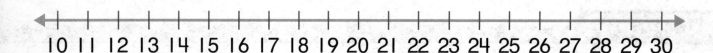

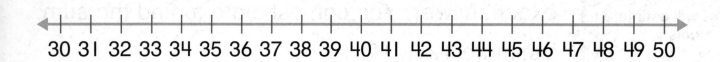

4. 11 + 47

11 rounds to ____

47 rounds to ____

____ + ____ = ____

5. 23 + 38

23 rounds to ____

38 rounds to ____

____ + ____ = ____

6. 14 + 28

14 rounds to ____

28 rounds to ____

____ + ____ = ____

7. 43 + 27

43 rounds to ____

27 rounds to ____

____ + ____ = ____

Problem Solving

8. Estimating Bubbles cost 40¢. Javon has 21 pennies and Cris has 23 pennies. Estimate. Do they have enough money to buy the bubbles? _____

Math at Home Activity: Have your child explain how to estimate 53 + 17.

Name _____

Add or subtract.

1. 4 tens + 2 tens = _____ tens   40 + 20 = _____

2. 6 tens + 1 ten = _____ tens   60 + 10 = _____

3. 5 tens − 2 tens = _____ tens   50 − 20 = _____

4. 7 tens − 3 tens = _____ tens   70 − 30 = _____

Add.

5.

tens	ones
2	2
+	3

6.

tens	ones
5	2
+	6

7.

tens	ones
6	2
+ 1	4

8.

tens	ones
6	1
+ 1	8

9. Vito has 36¢. A plastic ring costs 5¢.
Estimate. Does he have enough
money to buy two rings?

_____

Spiral Review Chapters 1–15

Write the addition sentence.

10.

_____ ◯ _____ ◯ _____

11.

_____ ◯ _____ ◯ _____

Skip count by 2s, 5s, or 10s.

12.

_____, _____, _____, _____   lemon seeds

13.

_____, _____, _____, _____, _____, _____   melon seeds

14.

_____, _____, _____, _____, _____   grapefruit seeds

Show the same amount of money in a different way.

	One Way	Another Way
15.	12¢	
16.	15¢	

Formative Assessment

Name _____

Subtract with Two-Digit Numbers

Main Idea

I will subtract from a two-digit number.

Find 25 − 4.

Step 1
Show the number.

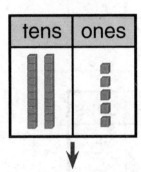

tens	ones
2	5
−	4

Step 2
Subtract the ones

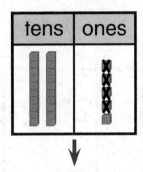

tens	ones
2	5
−	4
	1

Step 3
Subtract the tens.

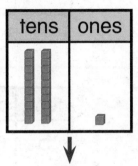

tens	ones
2	5
−	4
2	1

Check

Use WorkMat 7 and ▭▭▭▭▭▭ and ▪ . Subtract.

1.

tens	ones
1	7
−	3

2.

tens	ones
4	6
−	6

3.

tens	ones
3	7
−	2

4. (Talk About It) Which do you subtract first, tens or ones?

Use WorkMat 7 and ▭▭▭▭▭▭ and ▪ . Subtract.

5.

tens	ones
2	9
−	3

6.

tens	ones
6	7
−	3

7.

tens	ones
4	8
−	4

8.

tens	ones
5	4
−	2

9.

tens	ones
6	5
−	3

10.

tens	ones
9	3
−	2

11.

tens	ones
2	6
−	2

12.

tens	ones
7	7
−	5

13.

tens	ones
8	8
−	7

Problem Solving

14. Number Sense

Write a number sentence that shows
two numbers with a difference of 30.

_____ ◯ _____ ◯ _____

 Math at Home Activity: Have your child explain how to find 48 − 4.

Name _____

Subtract Two-Digit Numbers

Main Idea

I will subtract two-digit numbers.

Find 74 – 51.

Step 1	Step 2	Step 3
Show the number 74.	Subtract the ones.	Subtract the tens.

Step 1

tens	ones

↓

tens	ones
7	4
− 5	1

Step 2

tens	ones

↓

tens	ones
7	4
− 5	1
	3

Step 3

tens	ones

↓

tens	ones
7	4
− 5	1
2	3

Check

Use WorkMat 7 and 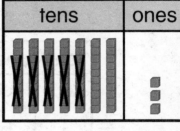 and ◼ . Subtract.

1.

tens	ones
2	8
− 1	5

2.

tens	ones
6	1
− 5	0

3.

tens	ones
3	4
− 1	4

4. **Talk About It** What goes in the tens place of the difference if you subtract all of the tens? For example: 66 – 64.

Use WorkMat 7 and ▭▭▭▭▭ and ▪ . Subtract

5.

tens	ones
5	8
− 1	3

6.

tens	ones
4	7
− 2	3

7.

tens	ones
4	4
− 1	1

8.

tens	ones
6	9
− 1	5

9.

tens	ones
9	4
− 2	1

10.

tens	ones
3	9
− 1	2

11.

tens	ones
9	4
− 2	1

12.

tens	ones
5	5
− 1	4

13.

tens	ones
8	2
− 1	2

Problem Solving

14. Number Sense Ricardo has
30 cards in one box
and 20 cards in another box.
He gives 10 cards to Rex.

How many cards does he have now? _____ cards

 Math at Home Activity: Have your child explain how to find 93 − 51.

Name _____

Problem-Solving Investigation

Main Idea

I will choose a strategy to solve a problem.

Your Mission:
Find out how many marbles in all.

I have 14 marbles. My sister has 24 marbles. How many marbles do we have altogether?

Understand

What do I know?
Underline what you know.

What do I need to find?
Circle it.

Plan

How will I solve the problem?
One way is to make a table.

Solve

Make a table.

Name	Tens	Ones
Mariah		
Sister		
Total:		

The girls have _____ marbles in all.

Check

Look back.
Is my answer reasonable?

Choose a strategy. Solve.

1. 13 children had dogs. 21 children had either a fish or a hamster. How many children had pets in all? _____ children

---

2. Isaiah started with 12 peas and 5 beans on his plate. Later he had 6 peas left on his plate. How many peas and beans has Isaiah eaten so far?

_____ peas and beans

---

3. 66 children can be seated on the school bus. After Emily got on, there were 42 children on the bus. How many more children can get on the bus?

_____ children

---

4. The library had 38 magazines. 12 students each checked out 2 magazines. How many magazines were left?

_____ magazines

Math at Home Activity: Take advantage of problem-solving opportunities during daily routines such as riding in the car, bedtime, doing laundry, putting away groceries, planning schedules, and so on.

Name _____

Estimate Differences

Main Idea

I will estimate differences.

Sometimes when you subtract, you do not need an exact answer. You can estimate to find the difference.

Estimate 32 − 21.

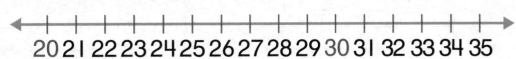

20 21 22 23 24 25 26 27 28 29 30 31 32 33 34 35

Step 1: Round to the nearest 10.

32 is closer to 30 ⟶ 32 rounds to 30.

21 is closer to 20 ⟶ 21 rounds to 20.

Step 2: Subtract.

30 − 20 = 10

3 − 2 = 1, so
30 − 20 = 10

Check

Round each number to the nearest ten.
Then subtract.

1. 79 − 41

79 rounds to _____

41 rounds to _____

_____ − _____ = _____

2. 64 − 37

64 rounds to _____

37 rounds to _____

_____ − _____ = _____

3.  **Talk About It** Explain how you would estimate 42 − 21.

Round each number to the nearest ten.
Then subtract.

4. 91 − 29

91 rounds to _____

29 rounds to _____

_____ − _____ = _____

5. 41 − 12

41 rounds to _____

12 rounds to _____

_____ − _____ = _____

6. 54 − 28

54 rounds to _____

28 rounds to _____

_____ − _____ = _____

7. 49 − 37

49 rounds to _____

37 rounds to _____

_____ − _____ = _____

8. 58 − 26

58 rounds to _____

26 rounds to _____

_____ − _____ = _____

9. 42 − 28

42 rounds to _____

28 rounds to _____

_____ − _____ = _____

10. **WRITING IN ►MATH** Why is 40 a better estimate
than 30 for 59 − 21?

_____

_____

_____

_____

Math at Home Activity: Have your child estimate 82 − 27 and then
explain his or her reasoning.

D

There were 38 marshmallows in the bag. Seth got hungry. He ate 6 marshmallows. How many marshmallows are left?

_____ marshmallows

FOLD DOWN

A

Problem Solving
in Social Sciences

Real-World MATH

You need to take many things on a camping trip. Lists make it easy to remember what to take!

This book belongs to

_____

Tabatha took 11 hot dogs. Brad took 7 hot dogs.
How many hot dogs did they take?

_____ hot dogs

Reba took 10 bottles of water.
Awan took 14 bottles of water.
How much water did Reba and Awan take?

_____ bottles of water

Name _____

Vocabulary

Complete the sentences.

1. When you do not need an exact answer you can _____ .

2. You _____ to the nearest 10.

Concepts

Add or subtract.

3. 6 tens + 2 tens = _____ tens   60 + 20 = _____

4. 5 tens − 2 tens = _____ tens   50 − 20 = _____

Add.

5.

tens	ones
9	3
+	5

6.

tens	ones
7	6
+ 1	3

7.

tens	ones
1	4
+ 2	5

Round each number to nearest ten. Then add.

40 41 42 43 44 45 46 47 48 49 50 51 52 53 54 55 56 57 58 59 60

8. 43 + 17

43 rounds to _____

17 rounds to _____

_____ + _____ = _____

9. 48 + 21

48 rounds to _____

21 rounds to _____

_____ + _____ = _____

Subtract.

10.

tens	ones
7	9
−	7

11.

tens	ones
8	6
−	5

12.

tens	ones
4	7
− 1	5

13.

tens	ones
6	7
− 1	3

Round each number to the nearest ten. Then subtract.

14. 57 − 26

57 rounds to _____

26 rounds to _____

_____ − _____ = _____

15. 94 − 36

94 rounds to _____

36 rounds to _____

_____ − _____ = _____

16. 88 − 16

88 rounds to _____

16 rounds to _____

_____ − _____ = _____

17. 19 − 11

19 rounds to _____

11 rounds to _____

_____ − _____ = _____

Problem Solving

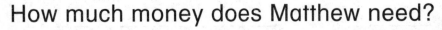

18. Matthew wants to buy two books.
Each book costs 23¢.
How much money does Matthew need? _____

Summative Assessment

Name _____

Listen as your teacher reads each problem.
Choose the correct answer.

1.

tens	ones
2	4
+ 3	0

34   36   50   54
○   ○   ○   ○

2.   43
        + 33

63   66   76   78
○   ○   ○   ○

3.

40 – 10 =   40 + 10 =

        ○   ○

10 – 40 =   10 + 40 =

        ○   ○

4. 33 – 23 =

50   40   20   10
○   ○   ○   ○

5.

35   30   25   20
○   ○   ○   ○

6. 3 – 3 = _____

3   2   1   0
○   ○   ○   ○

7.

$$\boxed{5, 10, 15, 20}$$

21, 22, 23   22, 24, 26
  ◯   ◯

25, 30, 35   30, 40, 50
  ◯   ◯

8.

66   65   55   46
◯   ◯   ◯   ◯

9. 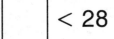 < 28

82   58   34   23
◯   ◯   ◯   ◯

10.

$$\boxed{9 + 9 = \underline{\hphantom{000}}}$$

0   9
◯   ◯

18   99
◯   ◯

11. There were 63 crows sitting on a fence. Then 30 flew away. How many crows are still on the fence?

_____ crows

12. Cole has a total of 18 cards in 2 boxes. She put 10 cards in one box. How many cards are in the second box?

_____ cards

Looking Ahead

Let's Look Ahead

Name _____

 ## Missing Addends

**Get Ready**

Main Idea

I will recall subtraction facts to help find missing addends.

Vocabulary

missing addend

You can use a related subtraction fact to help you find a **missing addend**.

$9 + \boxed{} = 13$

$13 - 9 = 4$

So $9 + \boxed{4} = 13$

4 is the missing addend.

I know 9 is one of the addends. The other addend is missing.

Check

Find the missing addend. Draw dots to help.

1.

$8 + \boxed{3} = 11 \quad 11 - 8 = \boxed{3}$

2.

$5 + \boxed{} = 12 \quad 12 - 5 = \boxed{}$

3.

$4 + \boxed{} = 9 \quad 9 - 4 = \boxed{}$

4.

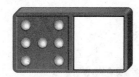

$7 + \boxed{} = 16 \quad 16 - 7 = \boxed{}$

5.  **Talk About It** How do you find the missing addend in

$6 + \boxed{} = 14?$

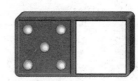

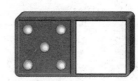

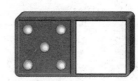

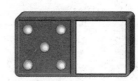

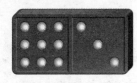
Find the missing addend.

6.

$12 - 9 = \boxed{}$

$9 + \boxed{} = 12$

7. $12 - 4 = \boxed{}$

$\boxed{} + 4 = 12$

8. $9 - 7 = \boxed{}$

$7 + \boxed{} = 9$

9. $12 - 6 = \boxed{}$

$6 + \boxed{} = 12$

10. $5 - 2 = \boxed{}$

$\boxed{} + 2 = 5$

11. $15 - \boxed{} = 6$

$6 + \boxed{} = 15$

12. $\boxed{} - 8 = 8$

$8 + \boxed{} = 16$

13.
$$\begin{array}{r} 7 \\ + \boxed{} \\ \hline 15 \end{array}$$

$$\begin{array}{r} 15 \\ - \boxed{} \\ \hline 7 \end{array}$$

14.
$$\begin{array}{r} 4 \\ + \boxed{} \\ \hline 13 \end{array}$$

$$\begin{array}{r} 13 \\ - \boxed{} \\ \hline 4 \end{array}$$

Problem Solving

15. Algebra There are 13 students with brown hair, red hair, or blonde hair. 7 have brown hair. 4 have red hair. How many have blonde hair?

$7 + 4 + \boxed{} = 13$ _____ students

 Math at Home Activity: Ask your child to tell you the subtraction fact that will help him or her add $7 + \boxed{} = 15$.

Name _____

② Count On Tens and Ones

Get Ready

Main Idea

I will count on by tens and ones to find sums.

Find 26 + 3.
Count on by ones.

26 + 3 = __29__

Find 26 + 30.
Count on by tens.

26 + 30 = __56__

Think
Start at 26.
Count 27, 28, 29.

Think
Start at 26.
Count 36, 46, 56.

✓ Check

Count on to add. Write the sum. Use 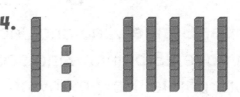 to help.

1.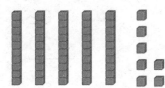

57 + 2 = __59__

2.

47 + 20 = ____

3.

13 + 3 = ____

4.

13 + 50 = ____

5. 3 + 24 = ____

6. 60 + 32 = ____

7. **Talk About It** How many tens do you count on to add 32 + 50? Explain.

Count on to add. Write the sum. Use ▭▭▭▭ to help.

8. 66 + 3 = _____

9. 14 + 70 = _____

10. 12 + 2 = _____

11. 25 + 3 = _____

12. 51 + 30 = _____

13. 45 + 10 = _____

14. 53 + 20 = _____

15. 3 + 12 = _____

16. 66 + 30 = _____

17. 51 + 5 = _____

18. 20 + 76 = _____

19. 32 + 1 = _____

20. 30 + 32 = _____

21. 3 + 32 = _____

22. 20 + 44 = _____

23. 3
    + 41

24. 10
    + 88

25. 1
    + 88

26. 32
    + 20

Problem Solving

27. Number Sense Zina and Jack each have 25 points. Zina scores 3 more points. How many points does Zina have now?

Zina has _____ points.

Jack gets 30 more points. How many points does Jack have now?

Jack has _____ points.

Math at Home Activity: Say a number between 10 and 50. Ask your child to count on by 1, 2, or 3 and then by 10, 20, or 30.

Name _____

 Hands-On Activity

 ③ Looking Ahead

Hundreds, Tens, and Ones

Get Ready

Main Idea

I will use hundreds, tens, and ones to show numbers.

There are 427 pennies in this jar. Use hundreds, tens and ones to show 427.

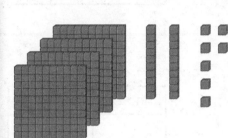

hundreds	tens	ones
4	2	7

427 four hundred twenty-seven.

✓ Check

Use base ten blocks to show each number. Write how many hundreds, tens, and ones. Then write the number.

1. Show 4 , 3 ▯, and 7 ◾.

hundreds	tens	ones

_____

2. Show 5 , I ▯, and 8 ◾.

hundreds	tens	ones

_____

3. **Talk About It** What is the value of the 2 in 712, 125, and 281?

Looking Ahead   Lesson 3

LA7

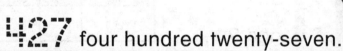

Use base ten blocks to show each number. Write how many hundreds, tens, and ones. Then write the number.

4. Show 3 ▦ , 8 ▮ , and 2 ▪ .

hundreds	tens	ones

_____

5. Show 2 ▦ , 8 ▮ , and 1 ▪ .

hundreds	tens	ones

_____

6. Show 7 ▦ , 0 ▮ , and 9 ▪ .

hundreds	tens	ones

_____

WRITING IN ▸MATH

7. Explain how many hundreds, tens, and ones 726 has. Draw it.

_____

_ _

_____

Math at Home Activity: Write the number 647. Ask your child to tell you how many hundreds, tens, and ones.

Name _____

4 Place Value to 1,000

Get Ready

Main Idea

I will use expanded form to write numbers up to 1,000.

Vocabulary

expanded form

Place value tells the value of a digit in a number.

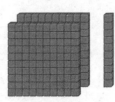

hundreds	tens	ones
2	1	3

Think
You can write a number in **expanded form**.

2 hundreds 1 ten 3 ones

$200 + 10 + 3$

213

✓ Check

Write the number in expanded form.
Then write the number.

1. 1 hundred 6 tens 2 ones

   ___ + ___ + ___

   ___

2. 1 hundred 2 tens 5 ones

   ___ + ___ + ___

   ___

Write the number.

3. $300 + 70 + 6 =$ _____

4. $700 + 60 + 1 =$ _____

Circle the value of the red digit.

5. 931

   300   30   3

6. 277

   200   20   2

7. **Talk About It** How are 762 and 267 the same?
   How are they different?

Write the number in expanded form.
Then write the number.

8. 6 hundreds 2 tens 5 ones

_____ + _____ + _____

_____

9. 9 hundreds 9 tens 9 ones

_____ + _____ + _____

_____

Write the number.

10. 600 + 30 + 8 = _____

11. 100 + 30 + 9 = _____

12 500 + 20 + 4 = _____

13. 200 + 70 + 2 = _____

Circle the value of the red digit.

14. 965

900   90   9

15. 673

300   30   3

16. 468

600   60   6

17. 890

800   80   8

H.O.T. Problem

18. **Make it Right**

Mario wrote 365 in expanded
form like this: 300 + 50 + 6.
Tell why Mario is wrong.
Then make it right.

300 + 50 + 6

_____

_____ + _____ + _____

Math at Home Activity: Have your child tell you a three digit number.
Then ask your child to tell you the value of the first digit.

Name _____

 # Measure to the Nearest Inch

Get Ready

Main Idea

I will use an inch ruler to measure.

Vocabulary

inch

Use an **inch** ruler to measure length.

First, line up the object with the end of the ruler starting at zero.

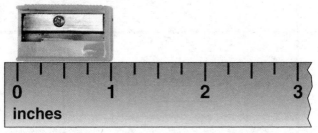

0 1 2 3
inches

Next, look at the marks on the ruler. Find the measurement that is closest to the end of the object.

This pencil sharpener is about

_____ inch long.

Check

Find the object. Estimate. Then use an inch ruler to measure.

Find	Estimate	Measure
1. 	about _____ inches	about _____ inches
2.	about _____ inches	about _____ inches

3. **Talk About It** Describe how you use an inch ruler to measure.

Find the object. Estimate. Measure to the
nearest inch.

Remember
Line up the object
with the end of
the ruler.

Find	Estimate	Measure
4. Dictionary	about _____ inches	about _____ inches
5.	about _____ inches	about _____ inches
6.	about _____ inches	about _____ inches
7. Chalkboard Eraser	about _____ inches	about _____ inches
8.	about _____ inches	about _____ inches

Problem Solving

9. **Thinking Math** A large paper clip is about
2 inches long. How long is a chain of 4 paper
clips?

about _____ inches

 Math at Home Activity: Ask your child to show you how to measure
the length of a piece of yarn or string with an inch ruler.

Name _____

 6 **Measure to the Nearest Centimeter**

Get Ready

Main Idea

I will use a centimeter ruler to measure.

Vocabulary

centimeter

Use a **centimeter** ruler to measure shorter objects.

First, line up the object with the end of the centimeter ruler starting at zero.

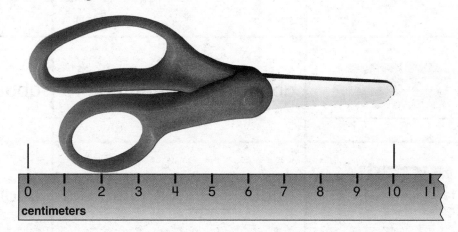

Next, look at the marks on the ruler. Find the measurement that is closest to the end of the object.

The scissors are about __10__ centimeters long.

✓ Check

Find the object. Estimate. Then use a centimeter ruler to measure.

Find	Estimate	Measure
1. 	about _____ centimeters	about _____ centimeters
2. ▬▬▬▬▬	about _____ centimeters	about _____ centimeters

3. **Talk About It** Would you use centimeters to measure the playground? Explain.

Estimate. Then use a centimeter ruler to measure.

Find	Estimate	Measure
4.	about _____ centimeters	about _____ centimeters
5.	about _____ centimeters	about _____ centimeters
6. Glue Stick	about _____ centimeters	about _____ centimeters
7.	about _____ centimeters	about _____ centimeters
8.	about _____ centimeters	about _____ centimeters

Problem Solving

9. Thinking Math About how many centimeters long is this toy truck? Write your answer.

_____ centimeters

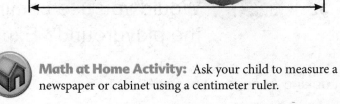

Math at Home Activity: Ask your child to measure a newspaper or cabinet using a centimeter ruler.

Problem-Solving Projects

End-of-Year Projects

Name: _____

You will find patterns in board games. You will also make your own board game.

Day 1: Can you find the pattern? ·····················

1. Look for a pattern on the board games. Describe it.

_____

_____

_____

_____

2. Identify the pattern unit on the board. Color the pattern below.

Day 2: Moving Forward

3. Find a partner. Take turns rolling the  15 times.

4. Make a bar graph to show your data.

What We Rolled												
	1	2	3	4	5	6	7	8	9	10	11	12

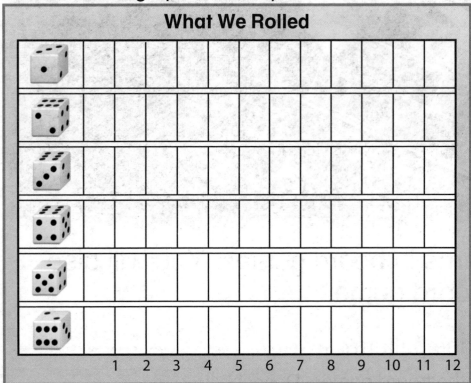

5. What number did you roll the greatest number of times? _____

6. What number did you roll the least number of times? _____

I Spy Patterns!

Day 3: Design your own board game.

7. Create a pattern on the game board.

8. Cut and paste the game squares onto the board.

9. Use  to move forward.

You will need:

Game squares:

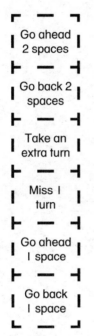

Go ahead 2 spaces

Go back 2 spaces

Take an extra turn

Miss 1 turn

Go ahead 1 space

Go back 1 space

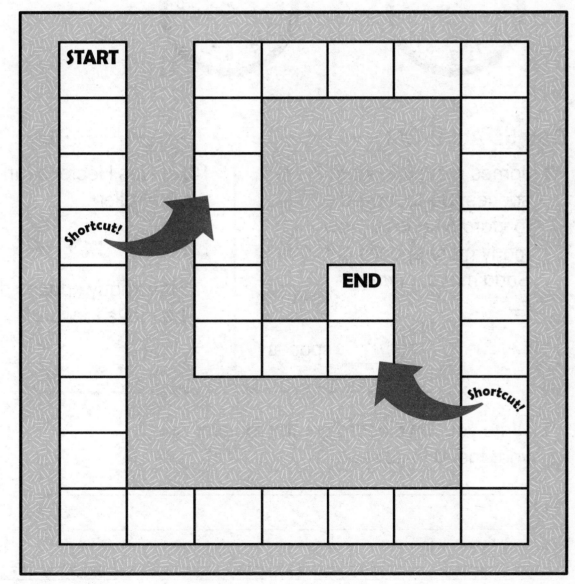

START

Shortcut!

END

Shortcut!

Day 4: Game Day!

10. Exchange your board game with a partner.

11. How long does it take to play your game? Draw the hands on the clocks.

Start

Finish

Day 5: Act It Out

12. James moved forward 2 spaces. Sada moved forward 6 spaces. How many more spaces did Sada move forward?

_____ spaces

13. It was Héctor's turn. He rolled:

How many spaces did he move forward?

_____ spaces

14. Write your own board game problem. Ask your friend to solve.

_____

_ _ _ _ _ _ _ _ _ _ _ _ _ _ _

_____

_ _ _ _ _ _ _ _ _ _ _ _ _ _ _

_____

I Spy Patterns!

Name: _____

Fruit Kabob Factory

PROJECT 2

You will make fruit kabobs in your classroom's factory.

Day 1: Which type of fruit is best to sell?

1. Ask 10 people to choose the fruit they like the best.

2. Organize your data in a tally chart.

Favorite Fruit		
Type of Fruit	Tally	Total

3. Make a picture graph to show your data.

Favorite Fruit

4. Circle the fruit you should use to make the fruit kabobs.

Day 2: Design your kabob ···

    5. Create patterns with different kinds of fruit.

    6. Draw your patterns.

> *Remember to use the fruits people liked the most.*

_____

_____

_____

    7. Circle the pattern that your team will make.

    8. Make a sign to show your product. Also tell people why they should buy your fruit kabob.

Day 3: It's time to buy supplies and pick a price. ·······················

    9. Look at the fruit kabob pattern your team will make. Write the supplies your group needs to buy.

_____

_ _ _ _ _ _ _ _ _ _ _ _ _ _ _ _

_____
_____

_ _ _ _ _ _ _ _ _ _ _ _ _ _ _ _

_____

   10. Look in store ads to find the prices of the ingredients.

   11. Draw the coins you used. Write the amount.

_____ ¢

   12. How much will you charge for your fruit kabob?

_____ ¢

Day 4: Get to work! ··

13. Draw the steps for making your fruit kabobs.

First	Second
Third	**Fourth**

14. Circle the step that takes the longest amount of time.

Day 5: Managers' Meeting

15. Explain how your team chose a price for your fruit kabobs.

16. Draw coins to show the price of your fruit kabobs.

One Way	Another Way

17. Each apple is 10¢.
How many apples can you buy with 90¢?

_______ apples

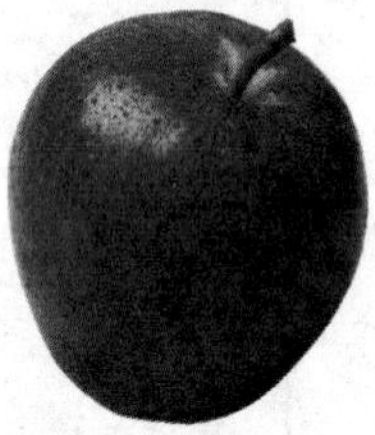

18. Oranges are 2 for 25¢.
How many oranges can you buy with 75¢?

_______ oranges

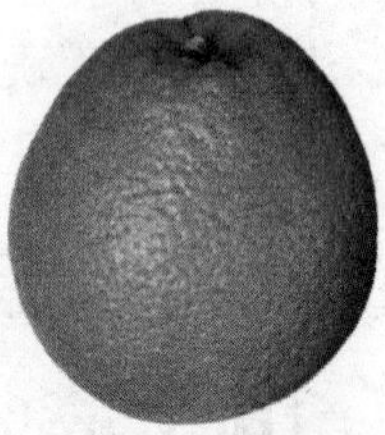

Name: _____

PROJECT 3

Let's Go to the Zoo!

I will plan a trip to the zoo.

Day 1: What animals will you see?

1. Ask 10 classmates to vote for their favorite animal.

2. Make a bar graph to show your data.

Favorite Animal									
Bear									
Lion									
Elephant									
Giraffe									

Let's Go to the Zoo!

Day 2: Let's plan our day. ....

3. Look at the bar graph you made.

4. List the animals in the order your class will see them.

First

_____

– – – – – – – – – – – – – – – – – – –

_____

Second

_____

– – – – – – – – – – – – – – – – – – –

_____

Third

_____

– – – – – – – – – – – – – – – – – – –

_____

Fourth

_____

– – – – – – – – – – – – – – – – – – –

_____

5. Use the *Zoo Trip Schedule* to complete the chart on the next page.

Zoo Trip Schedule

- You will arrive at the zoo at 9:00.

- You will see the first animal a half hour after you arrive.

- You will leave the zoo at 1:00.

- You will see the fourth animal a half hour before you leave the zoo.

- You will eat lunch 2 hours before you leave the zoo.

- You will see the second animal a half hour after you see the first animal.

- You will see the third animal a half hour before lunch.

Let's Go to the Zoo!

6. Use the zoo trip schedule on P12. Draw hands on the clocks to match the times on the schedule. Write the activity.

Zoo Trip Schedule		
9:00		
9:30		
10:00		
10:30	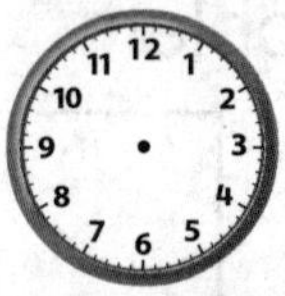	
11:00		
12:30		
1:00		

Day 3: Zoo Lunch Budget ·

7. Each student can have $\frac{1}{4}$ of a pizza. Draw a picture to solve. How many pizzas will your class need to order?

_____ pizzas

8. Each pizza costs 5 dollars. Count by 5's to find the total cost of the pizzas. Write the amount.

_____ dollars

9. You received the first grader discount! The pizzas are 2 dollars each. Write the new amount.

_____ dollars

Day 4: How will you get to the zoo?

10. If each van can hold 6 people, how many vans will you need to take? _____ vans Use counters and the boxes below to solve the problem.

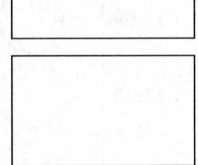
Don't forget your teacher!

Day 5: Design your own zoo.

11. On a separate piece of paper, draw a map of a zoo.

12. Draw hands on the clock to show when your zoo will open and close.

Zoo Hours

Open   Close

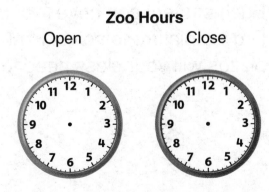

Let's Go to the Zoo!

Name: _____

PROJECT 4

Toys From the Past and Present

You will compare toys and games from the past and present.

Day 1: Compare prices

1. Use coins to show each amount.
   Draw the coins you used.

Past	Present
5¢	79¢

Toys From the Past and Present

2. Use coins to show each amount. Draw the coins you used.

Past	Present
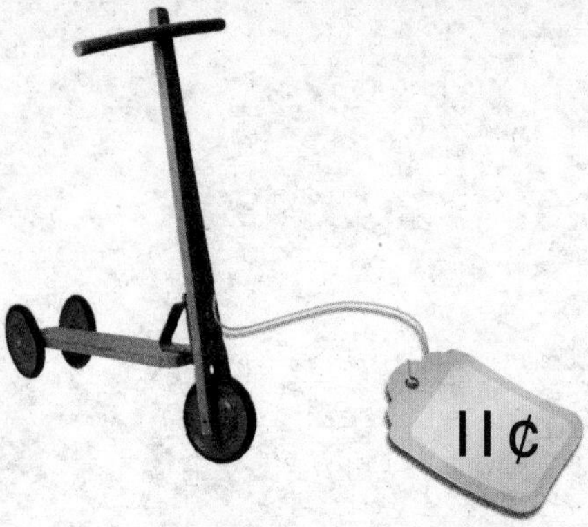 11¢	 99¢
 8¢	 92¢

Toys From the Past and Present

Day 2: Make your own puzzle

3. Look at the puzzle. Draw a pattern in each row.

Puzzles have been around for a long time. Did you know you can make your own?

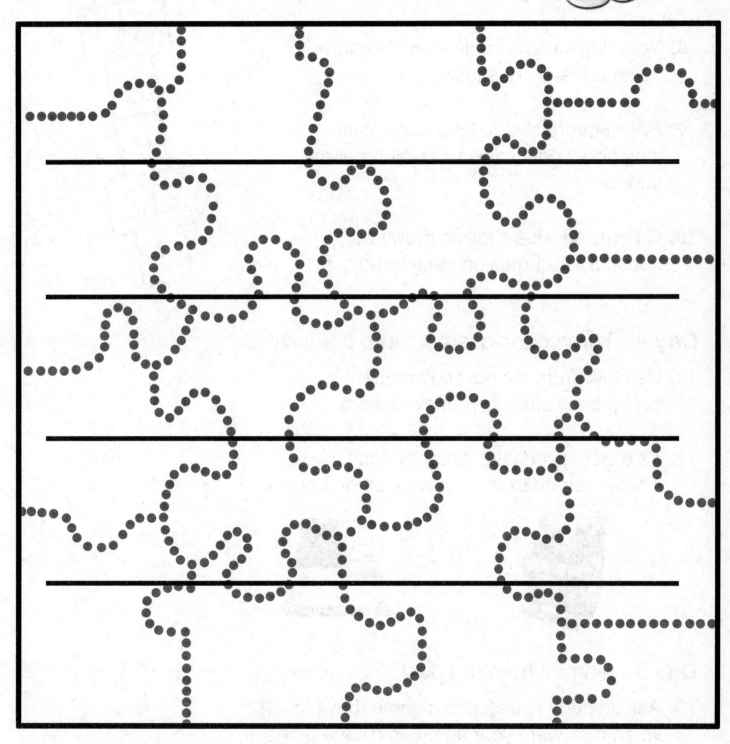

4. Describe your patterns to a friend.

5. Cut along the dotted lines to make puzzle pieces. Put them in a plastic bag.

6. Give your puzzle to a friend to put together.

Toys From the Past and Present

Day 3: Make your own outdoor game.

7. Design a hopscotch game. Draw squares on a separate sheet of paper.

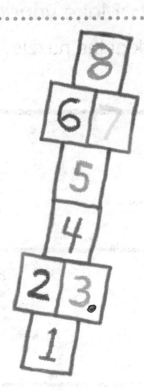

8. Your hopscotch should have 8 squares, 10 squares, or 12 squares.

9. Each square should be 2 paper clips long and 2 paperclips wide. Number the squares.

10. Go outside. Use chalk to draw your hopscotch squares on the ground.

Day 4: Turn your classroom into a toy store.

11. Use toys from the past and present to set up a toy store in your classroom.

12. As a class, choose a price for each toy. Then, pretend to shop or work at the toy store.

Day 5: Games from the past.

13. Ask an adult to describe a game they played when they were your age. Explain the game to a friend.

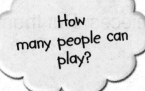
How many people can play?

Do you play it indoors or outdoors?

Do you need a ball to play the game?

Toys From the Past and Present

Student Handbook

Built-In Workbook

Reference

How to Use the Student Handbook

Use the Student Handbook

You, or your teacher, may decide that working through some additional problems would be helpful. The **Facts Practice** section is useful:

- when you need more practice with addition facts and subtraction facts
- when you need to show different ways to make numbers, show the order of numbers, count on to add, count back to subtract, or write numbers as hundreds, tens, and ones
- when you need to know the meaning of a math word
- when you need to find number patterns, to order numbers, or to skip count
- when you need help writing the number names

Concepts and Skills Bank

Name _____

① True and False Statements

In math, statements can be true or false.

A true statement is correct.

$5 + 1 = 6$ is **true**

A false statement is incorrect.

$5 + 1 = 5$ is **false**

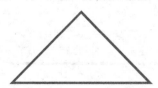 **Practice**

Circle true or false.

1. This is a triangle.

true   false

2. 8 is greater than 2
  true   false

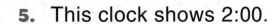
Circle true or false.

3. $13 + 3 = 43$

   true   false

4. $23 - 10 = 13$

   true   false

5. This clock shows 2:00.

   true   false

6. This clock shows 9:00.

   true   false

7. Write your own true math statement.

_____

- -

_____

8. Write your own false math statement.

_____

- -

_____

Concepts and Skills

Concepts and Skills Bank

Name _____

2 Half Dollars and Dollars

A dollar has a value of 100 cents. A half dollar
has a value of 50 cents.

When you write one dollar, use a dollar sign
and a decimal point.

dollar sign ——→ $1.00
                        ↑
                  decimal point

100 pennies = $1.00	20 nickels = $1.00	10 dimes = $1.00	4 quarters = $1.00	2 half dollars = $1.00

1. Mika needs $1.00 to buy some erasers.
   Here are the coins Mika has.

How much money does Mika have? _____

Does she have enough money for the erasers?

yes   no

2. Emilio needs $1.00 to buy a pencil.
   Here are the coins Emilio has.

How much money does Emilio have? _____

Does he have enough money for the pencil?

yes   no

3. Tessa needs $1.00 to buy a yo-yo.
   Here are the coins Tessa has.

How much money does Tessa have? _____

Does she have enough money for the yo-yo?

yes   no

Concepts and Skills Bank

Name _____

3 Symmetry and Congruence

Figures that are the same size and shape are congruent.

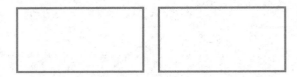

A figure has a line of symmetry if it can be folded in half and the two halves are congruent.

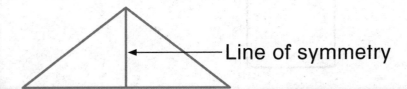
Line of symmetry

Practice

Circle the shape that is congruent.

1.

   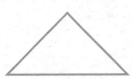

Draw a line of symmetry.

2.

Circle the shape that is congruent.

3.

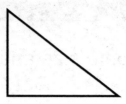

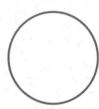

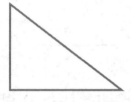

4.

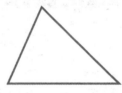

Draw a line of symmetry.

5.

6.

Concepts and Skills

Concepts and Skills Bank

Name _____

4 Perimeter

Perimeter is the sum of all the sides.

$4 + 4 + 4 + 4 = 16$

The perimeter is 16.

Perimeter can be used to find the distance around an object.

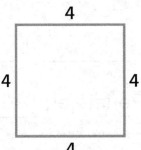

▶ Practice

Find the perimeter.

1.

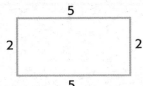

_____ + _____ + _____ + _____ = _____

Perimeter: _____

2.

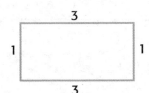

_____ + _____ + _____ + _____ = _____

Perimeter: _____

3.

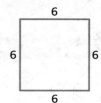

_____ + _____ + _____ + _____ = _____

Perimeter: _____

4.

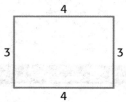

_____ + _____ + _____ + _____ = _____

Perimeter: _____

5.

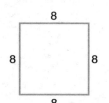

_____ + _____ + _____ + _____ = _____

Perimeter: _____

6.

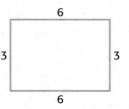

_____ + _____ + _____ + _____ = _____

Perimeter: _____

Concepts and Skills

Concepts and Skills Bank

Name _____

5 Temperature

A thermometer is used to measure temperature.

The red shows the temperature.

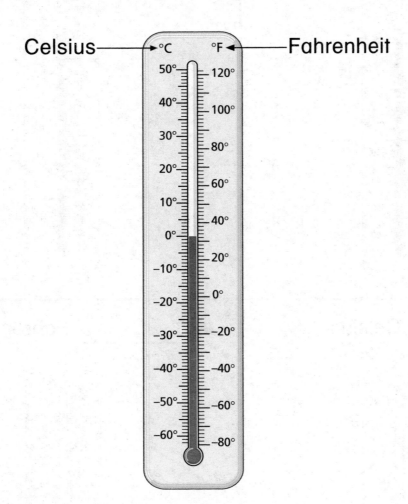

Celsius → °C   °F ← Fahrenheit

This thermometer shows 32°F and 0°C.

Practice

Write the temperature.

1. _____ Fahrenheit

2. _____ Celsius

3. _____ Celsius

4. _____ Fahrenheit

Preparing for Standardized Tests

It's time to review how to take a standardized test. You have been building your math skills in class. Soon you will have a chance to put them to work.

Tips for Success!

Before a Test

- Go to bed early the night before.
- Eat a good breakfast the next morning.

During a Test

- Listen carefully as your teacher reads each question.
- Work carefully.

Whatever you do...

- Do not rush.
- Do not give up.

RELAX. Just do your best.

Multiple-Choice

You will fill in bubbles to answer questions.

Make sure to:
- Fill in the bubble completely.
- Make your marks dark.
- If you make a mistake, erase it all.

Correct			
2	5	7	9
⬭	⬭	⬤	⬭

Not Correct			
2	5	7	9
⬭	⬭	⊙	⬭

Short-Response

You will solve problems and write your answers on the line.

Make sure to:
- Work slowly and carefully.
- Use your neatest handwriting.
- Check your work.
- Make sure that you answered the question.

Name _____

Multiple-Choice Practice

Directions

Listen as your teacher reads each problem.
Choose the correct answer.

1. There are twenty-two cows
   on a farm. There are nine
   pigs. About how many
   animals are there in all?

   about 10   about 20
      ○   ○

   about 25   about 30
      ○   ○

2. Jeremy has thirty-one
   crayons. Ana has fifty-two
   crayons. About how many
   more crayons does Ana
   have than Jeremy?

   about 10   about 20
      ○   ○

   about 25   about 30
      ○   ○

3. Which sign makes the
   number sentence true?

   $$9 - 5 \boxed{} 4$$

   +   =   >   <
   ○   ○   ○   ○

4. Three bees are on a flower.
   Four more bees join them.
   Which number sentence
   shows how many bees there
   are in all?

   $4 + 3 = 7$ $4 - 3 = 1$
      ○   ○

   $3 + 3 = 6$ $7 - 4 = 3$
      ○   ○

5. What time is shown on the
   clock?

   3 o'clock   6 o'clock
      ○   ○

   9 o'clock   10 o'clock
      ○   ○

6. Which activity takes the most
   time?

   ○   brushing your teeth

   ○   watching a movie

   ○   walking a dog

   ○   taking a bath

Multiple-Choice Practice

Directions

Listen as your teacher reads each problem.
Choose the correct answer.

7. What shape makes up the faces of the figure below?

circle ○   line ○

square ○   triangle ○

8. What is the name of this figure?

circle ○   rectangle ○

square ○   triangle ○

9. What rule could you use to find the next number in the pattern?

1, 3, 5, 7, 9, 11, 13, 15

add 1 ○   subtract 1 ○

add 2 ○   subtract 2 ○

10. Kareem made a number pattern showing the amount of money in nickels. What is the next amount of money in the pattern?

5¢, 10¢, 15¢, 20¢, 25¢, 30¢

30¢ ○   35¢ ○   40¢ ○   45¢ ○

11. Look at the number below. How do you read this number?

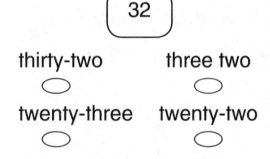

32

thirty-two ○   three two ○

twenty-three ○   twenty-two ○

12. Look at the numbers below. What can you replace the blank with to make a true statement?

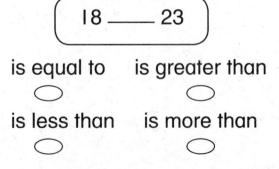

18 ____ 23

is equal to ○   is greater than ○

is less than ○   is more than ○

Name _____

Short-Response Practice

Directions

Listen as your teacher reads each problem.
Write the correct answer.

1. Jenny has 4 pencils. She buys 3 more at the store. How many pencils does she have in all?

_____ pencils

2. Kiah put eleven beads on a bracelet. Then she added twenty-one more beads. About how many beads did she use?

about _____ beads

3. Megan's family has 3 dogs and 2 cats. How many pets do they have in all?

_____ pets

4. Amy skipped rope sixty-two times at recess. Michael skipped rope eighteen times. About how many more times did Amy skip rope than Michael?

about _____ times

5. Andy had ten colored pencils. He gave four of them to Marta. Write a number sentence to show how many colored pencils Andy has left.

_____

6. Vicky's school begins at the time shown on the clock. What time is shown on the clock?

_____

Short-Response Practice

Directions

Listen as your teacher reads each problem.
Write the correct answer.

7. What is the value of this coin?

_____ ¢

8. What shape is this party hat?

_____

9. What is this shape?

_____

10. Miles had nine tennis balls. He gave two of them to Matthew. Write a number sentence to show how many tennis balls Miles has left.

_____

11. Name the shape that comes next in this pattern.

_____

12. What rule could you use to find the next number in the pattern?

4, 5, 6, 7, 8, 9, 10, 11, 12

_____

13. Look at the pattern of numbers below. Which number comes next?

10, 20, 30, 40

_____

14. What rule could you use to find the next number in the pattern?

3, 6, 9, 12, 15

_____

Glossary/Glosario

English		Español
	A	

add (adding, addition) To join together sets to find the total or sum. (page 53)

$$2 + 5 = 7$$

sumar (suma, adición) Unir conjuntos para hallar el total o la suma.

$$2 + 5 = 7$$

---

addend Any numbers or quantities being added together. (page 155)

$$2 + 3$$

2 is an addend and 3 is an addend.

sumando Números o cantidades que se suman.

$$2 + 3$$

2 es un sumando y 3 es un sumando.

---

addition sentence An expression using numbers and the + and = signs. (page 55)

$$4 + 5 = 9$$

expresión de suma Expresión que usa números y los signos + y =.

$$4 + 5 = 9$$

---

after To follow in place or time. (page 39)

6 is just *after* 5

después Que sigue en lugar o en tiempo.

5 **6** 7 8

6 viene inmediatemente *después* del 5

Glossary/Glosario

English	**Español**

afternoon A time in the day between noon and sunset. (page 213)

tarde Momento del día entre el mediodía y el atardecer.

afternoon

tarde

analog A clock that has an hour hand and a minute hand. (page 223)

analógico Reloj que tiene manecilla horaria y minutero.

minute hand — hour hand

minutero — manecilla horaria

B

bar graph A graph that uses bars to show data.

(page 133)

gráfica de barras Gráfica que usa barras para mostrar datos.

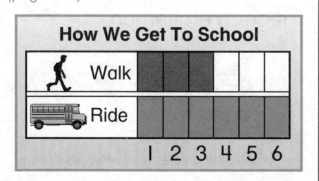

How We Get To School
Walk
Ride
1 2 3 4 5 6

Cómo Vamos a la Escuela
Caminando
En automóvil
1 2 3 4 5 6

Glossary/Glosario

	English	**B**	**Español**	

before
(page 39)

6 is just *before* 7

antes

6 viene inmediatamente *antes* del 7

between (page 39)

The kitten is *between* the two dogs.

entre

El gatito está *entre* dos perros.

C

cent ¢ (page 351)

1¢   1 cent

centavo ¢

1¢   1 centavo

English	**Español**

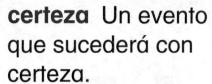

certain An event will happen for sure. (page 143)

certeza Un evento que sucederá con certeza.

circle A closed round figure. (page 395)

círculo Figura redonda y cerrada.

cold/colder/coldest (page 295)

cold

frío/más frío/ el más frío

frío

cone (page 385)

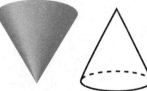

cono

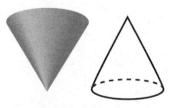

Glossary/Glosario

English		Español

English

corner The point where lines, edges, or sides of a figure meet. A corner is also called a *vertex*. (page 387)

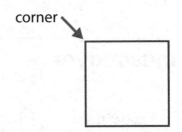

corner

Español

esquina Punto donde se unen las líneas, bordes o lados de una figura. Una esquina también se llama *vértice*.

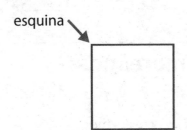

esquina

---

count back On a number line, start at the number 5 and count back 3. (page 185)

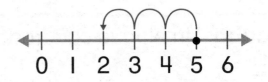

$5 - 3 = 2$ Count back 3.

contar hacia atrás En una fila de números, comienza en el número 5 y cuenta 3 hacia atrás.

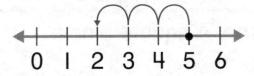

$5 - 3 = 2$ Cuenta 3 hacia atrás.

---

count on (or count up) On a number line, start at the number 4 and count up 2. (page 157)

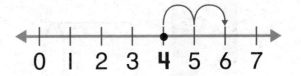

$4 + 2 = 6$ Count on 2.

contar hacia delante (o hacia arriba) En una fila de números, comienza en el número cuat ro y cuenta 2 hacia adelante.

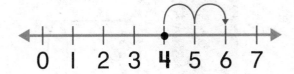

$4 + 2 = 6$ Cuenta 2 hacia adelante.

Glossary/Glosario

English	Español

covers less/least (page 301)

covers less

cubre menos/lo menor

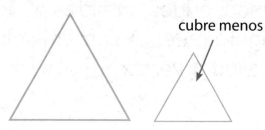

cubre menos

covers more/most
(page 301)

covers more

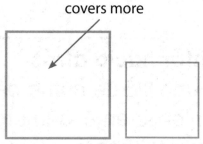

cubre más/mayor

cubre más

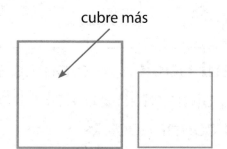

cube A square block.
(page 385)

 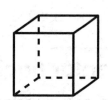

cubo Un bloque cuadrado.

 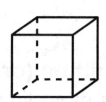

cylinder A solid figure shaped like a can. (page 385)

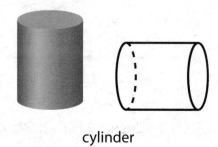

cylinder

cilindro Figura sólida en forma de lata.

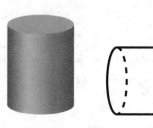

cilindro

Glossary/Glosario

English	Español

data Numbers or symbols collected to show information. (page 125)

datos Números o símbolos que se reúnen para mostrar información.

Name	Number of Pets
Mary	3
James	1
Alonzo	4

Nombre	Número de mascotas
Mary	3
James	1
Alonzo	4

difference The answer to a subtraction problem. (page 91)

diferencia Respuesta a un problema de resta.

$$3 - 1 = 2$$

The difference is 2. ↑

$$3 - 1 = 2$$

La diferencia es 2. ↑

digital A clock that uses only numbers to show time. (page 223)

digital Reloj que usa sólo números para mostrar la hora.

dime dime = 10¢ or 10 cents (page 353)

moneda de 10 centavos moneda de 10 centavos = 10¢ ó 10 centavos

head   tail

cara   escudo

English	**Español**
doubles (and doubles plus 1) Two addends that are the same number. (pages 169 and 171)	**dobles (y dobles más 1)** Dos sumandos que son el mismo número.
$2 + 2 = 4$ $2 + 3 = 5$	$2 + 2 = 4$ $2 + 3 = 5$
equal parts Each part is the same size. (page 457) A muffin cut in equal parts. 	**partes iguales** Cada parte es del mismo tamaño. Un panecillo cortado en partes iguales. 
equals (=) Having the same value as or is the same as. (page 55) $2 + 4 = 6$ equal sign ↑	**igual (=)** Que tienen el mismo valor o son iguales a. $2 + 4 = 6$ signo de igual ↑
estimate To find a number close to an exact amount. (page 255)	**estimar** Hallar un número cercano a la cantidad exacta.

Glossary/Glosario

English	**Español**

E

even Numbers that end with 0, 2, 4, 6, 8. (page 263)

par Números que terminan en 0, 2, 4, 6, 8.

---

evening The time after school when it is dark. (page 213)

anochecer Hora después de la escuela cuando está oscuro.

evening

anochecer

F

face The flat part of a 3-dimensional figure. (page 387)

cara Parte plana de una figura de 3 dimensiones.

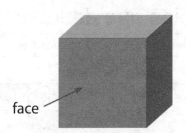

face

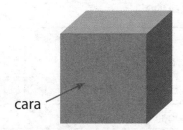

cara

Glossary/Glosario

English		Español

F

fact family Addition and subtraction sentences that use the same numbers. Sometimes called *related facts*. (page 199)

$$6 + 7 = 13 \quad 13 - 7 = 6$$
$$7 + 6 = 13 \quad 13 - 6 = 7$$

familia de datos Expresiones de suma y resta que utilizan los mismos números. Algunas veces se llaman *datos relacionados*.

$$6 + 7 = 13 \quad 13 - 7 = 6$$
$$7 + 6 = 13 \quad 13 - 6 = 7$$

fraction A number that represents part of a whole or part of a set. (page 461)

$$\frac{1}{2}, \frac{1}{3}, \frac{1}{4}, \frac{3}{4}$$

fracción Número que representa la parte de un todo o la parte de un conjunto.

$$\frac{1}{2}, \frac{1}{3}, \frac{1}{4}, \frac{3}{4}$$

G

graph A way to present data collected. Also a type of chart. (page 125)

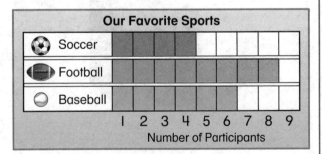

bar graph

gráfica Forma de presentar datos recogidos. También tipo de tabla.

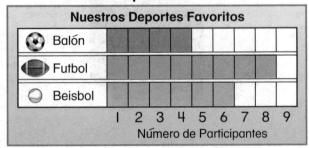

una gráfica de barras

English		Español
	H	

half hour (or half past)
One half of an hour is 30 minutes. Sometimes called *half past* or *half past the hour.* (page 217)

media hora (o y media)
Media hora son 30 minutos. Algunas veces se llama 'y media'.

heavy (heavier, heaviest)
Weighs more. (page 285)
An elephant is heavier than a mouse.

heavier

pesado (más pesado, el más pesado) Pesa más. Un elefante es más pesado (pesa más) que un ratón.

más pesado

holds less/least (page 291)

The glass holds less than the pitcher.

contener menos

El vaso contiene menos que la jarra.

Glossary/Glosario

English	H	Español

holds more/most (page 291)

The pitcher holds more than the glass.

contener más

El vaso contiene más que la jarra.

hot/hotter/hottest (page 295)

hot

caliente/más caliente/ el más caliente

caliente

hour A unit of time
1 hour = 60 minutes (page 215)

hora Unidad de tiempo.
1 hora = 60 minutos

hour hand The hand on a clock that tells the hour. It is the shorter hand. (page 215)

hour hand

manecilla horaria
Manecilla del reloj que dice la hora. Es la manecilla más corta.

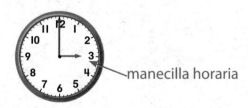

manecilla horaria

Glossary/Glosario

English		Español

English

hundred chart A chart that shows numbers 1–100.

(page 249)

1	2	3	4	5	6	7	8	9	10
11	12	13	14	15	16	17	18	19	20
21	22	23	24	25	26	27	28	29	30
31	32	33	34	35	36	37	38	39	40
41	42	43	44	45	46	47	48	49	50
51	52	53	54	55	56	57	58	59	60
61	62	63	64	65	66	67	68	69	70
71	72	73	74	75	76	77	78	79	80
81	82	83	84	85	86	87	88	89	90
91	92	93	94	95	96	97	98	99	100

Español

tabla de cien Tabla que muestra los números. 1–100.

1	2	3	4	5	6	7	8	9	10
11	12	13	14	15	16	17	18	19	20
21	22	23	24	25	26	27	28	29	30
31	32	33	34	35	36	37	38	39	40
41	42	43	44	45	46	47	48	49	50
51	52	53	54	55	56	57	58	59	60
61	62	63	64	65	66	67	68	69	70
71	72	73	74	75	76	77	78	79	80
81	82	83	84	85	86	87	88	89	90
91	92	93	94	95	96	97	98	99	100

I

impossible An event that cannot happen. (page 143)

You cannot pick a blue cube.

imposible Un evento que no puede ocurrir.

No puedes elegir un cubo azul.

is equal to = (page 35)

$$6 = 6$$
6 is equal to 6

igual a =

$$6 = 6$$
6 es igual a 6

Glossary/Glosario

English	**Español**

I

is greater than > (page 35)

7 > 2

7 is greater than 2

mayor que >

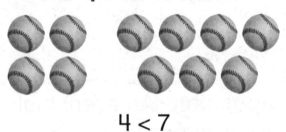

7 > 2

7 es mayor que 2

is less than < (page 35)

4 < 7

4 is less than 7

menor que <

4 < 7

4 es menor que 7

L

length (page 277)

length

longitud

longitud

Glossary/Glosario

English	**Español**

L

light (lighter, lightest)
Weighs less. (page 285)
The mouse is lighter than the elephant.

lighter

liviano (más liviano, el más liviano) Pesa menos.
El ratón es más liviano (pesa menos) que el elefante.

más liviano

---

long (longer, longest) A way to compare the lengths of two objects. (page 277)

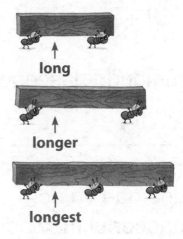

long

longer

longest

largo (más largo, el más largo) Forma de comparar la longitud de dos objetos.

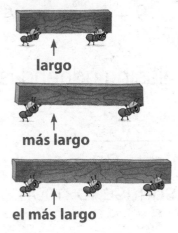

largo

más largo

el más largo

M

measure To find the length, height, or weight using standard or nonstandard units. (page 279)

medir Hallar la longitud, estatura o peso mediante unidades estándar o no estándar.

Glossary/Glosario

English	Español
M	

minus (−) The sign used to show subtraction.
(page 91)

$$5 - 2 = 3$$
minus sign

resta (−)
Signo que se usa en la resta.

$$5 - 2 = 3$$
signo de resta

minute hand The longer hand on a clock that tells the minutes. (page 215)

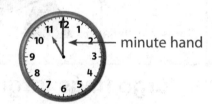
minute hand

minutero La manecilla más larga de un reloj que indica los minutos.

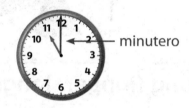
minutero

missing addend

$$9 + \underline{\quad} = 16$$

The missing addend is 7.

sumando desconocido

$$9 + \underline{\quad} = 16$$

El sumando desconocido es 7.

morning The period of time from sunrise to noon. (page 213)

morning

mañana Período de tiempo que va del amanecer al mediodía.

mañana

Glossary/Glosario

English		Español

nickel 5¢ or 5 cents (page 351)

moneda de cinco centavos 5¢ ó 5 centavos

head   tail

cara   escudo

---

number Tells how many.
1, 2, 3, 4, 5, 6, 7, 8, 9, 10, …
(page 23)

números Decir cuántos.
1, 2, 3, 4, 5, 6, 7, 8, 9, 10, …

There are 3 chicks.

Hay 3 pollito.

---

number line A line with number labels. (page 39)

línea de números Línea con rótulos de números.

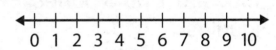

0 1 2 3 4 5 6 7 8 9 10

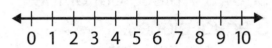

0 1 2 3 4 5 6 7 8 9 10

O

---

o'clock At the beginning of the hour. (page 215)

en punto Al comienzo de la hora.

It is 3 o'clock.

Son las 3 en punto.

---

odd Numbers that end with 1, 3, 5, 7, 9. (page 263)

impar Números que terminan en 1, 3, 5, 7, 9.

English	o	Español

one fourth A fraction that shows 1 piece out of 4 equal pieces. (page 463)

$\frac{1}{4}$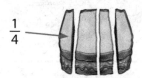

un cuarto Fracción que muestra 1 de 4 partes iguales.

$\frac{1}{4}$

one half A fraction that shows 1 piece out of 2 equal pieces.

(page 461)

$\frac{1}{2}$

un medio Fracción que muestra 1 de 2 partes iguales.

$\frac{1}{2}$

one third A fraction that shows 1 piece out of the 3 equal pieces. (page 463)

$\frac{1}{3}$

un tercio Fracción que muestra 1 de 3 partes iguales.

$\frac{1}{3}$

ones
This number has 3 ones. (page 243)

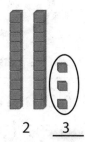

2   3

unidades
Este número tiene 3 unidades.

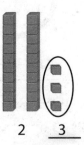

2   3

English ## Español

O

order

1, 3, 6, 7, 9 (page 39)

These numbers are in order from least to greatest.

orden

1, 3, 6, 7, 9

Estos números están en orden del menor al mayor.

P

pattern An order that a set of objects or numbers follows over and over. (page 17)

A, A, B, A, A, B, A, A, B

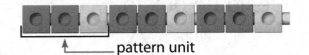

↑ pattern unit

patrón Orden que sigue continuamente un conjunto de objetos o números.

A, A, B, A, A, B, A, A, B

↑ unidad de patrón

penny 1¢ or 1 cent (page 351)

head   tail

moneda de un centavo

1¢ ó 1 centavo

cara   escudo

picture graph A graph that has different pictures to show information collected. (page 125)

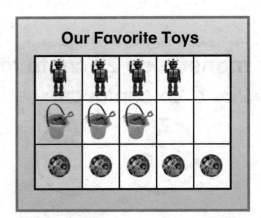

Our Favorite Toys

gráfica con imágenes Gráfica que tiene diferentes imágenes para mostrar la información recogida.

Nuestros Juguetes Favoritos

Glossary/Glosario

English 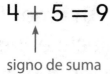	Español
plane figure See 2-dimensional figure. (page 395)	**figura plana** Ver figuras de 2 dimensiones.
plus (+) A symbol to show addition. (page 55) $$4 + 5 = 9$$ 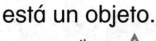 plus sign	**suma (+)** Símbolo para mostrar la suma. $$4 + 5 = 9$$ signo de suma
position Tell where an object is. (page 401) 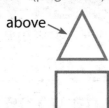 above	**posición** Dice dónde está un objeto. 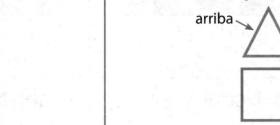 arriba
pyramid A solid figure with a polygon as a base and triangular shaped faces. (page 385) 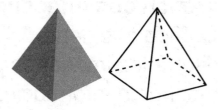	**pirámide** Figura sólida con un polígono como base y caras de forma triangular. 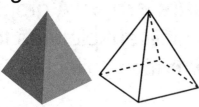

Q	
quarter 25¢ or 25 cents (page 365)  head tail	**moneda de 25 centavos** 25¢ ó 25 centavos cara escudo

Glossary/Glosario

English Español

rectangle A shape with four sides and four corners. (page 395) 	**rectángulo** Figura con cuatro lados y cuatro esquinas. 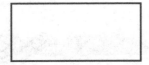
rectangular prism A 3-dimensional shape. (page 385)  rectangular prism	**prisma rectangular** Figura de 3 dimensiones. 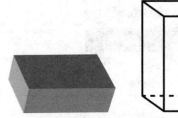 Prisma rectangular
regroup To take apart a number to write it in a new way. (page 423) 1 ten + 2 ones becomes 12 ones 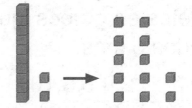	**reagrupar** Separar un número para escribirlo en una nueva forma. 1 decena + 2 unidades se convierten en 12 unidades. 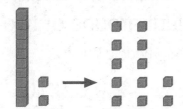
round To change the *value* of a number to one that is easier to work with. (page 495) 24 rounded to the nearest 10 is 20.	**redondear** Cambiar el *valor* de un número a uno con el que es más fácil trabajar. 24 redondeado a la decena más cercana es 20.

Glossary/Glosario

English	S	Español

short (shorter, shortest)
To compare length or height of two (or more) objects.
(page 277)

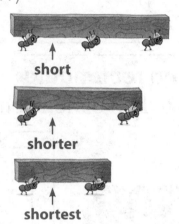

corto (más corto, el más corto) Comparar la longitud o la altura de dos (o más) objetos.

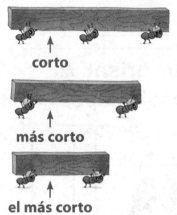

---

side (page 395)

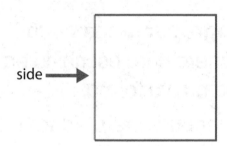

lado

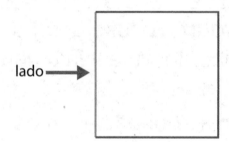

---

skip count To count objects in equal groups of two or more. (page 259)

2,4,6,8,10

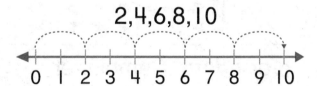

conteo en grupos Contar objetos en grupos iguales de dos o más.

2,4,6,8,10

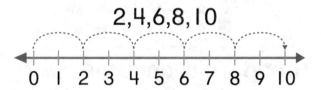

---

solid figure See 3-dimensional figure. (page 385)

figura sólida Ver figura de 3 dimensiones.

English	Español
sort To group together like items. (page 123)	**ordenar** Agrupar elementos iguales.

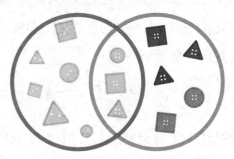

| **sphere** A solid figure that has the shape of a round ball. (page 367) | **esfera** Figura sólida con la forma de una pelota redonda. |

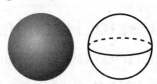

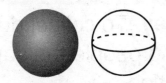

| **square** A rectangle that has four equal sides. (page 395) | **cuadrado** Rectángulo que tiene cuatro lados iguales. |

| **subtract (subtracting, subtraction)** To take away, take apart, separate, or find the difference between two sets. The opposite of addition. (page 89) | **restar (resta, sustracción)** Eliminar, quitar, separar o hallar la diferencia entre dos conjuntos. Lo opuesto de la suma. |

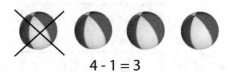

4 - 1 = 3

4 - 1 = 3

Glossary/Glosario

English		Español

subtraction sentence
An expression using numbers and the – and = signs. (page 91)

$$9 - 5 = 4$$

expresión de resta
Expresión que contiene números y los signos de – y =.

$$9 - 5 = 4$$

---

sum The answer to an addition problem. (page 55)

$$2 + 4 = 6$$
$$\uparrow$$
sum

suma Respuesta a un problema de suma.

$$2 + 4 = 6$$
$$\uparrow$$
suma

---

survey To collect data by asking people the same question. (page 129)

Favorite Foods	
Food	Votes
🍎	卌
🍌	|||
🥪	卌 |||

This survey shows favorite foods.

encuesta Recoger datos haciendo las mismas preguntas a las personas.

Comidas Favoritas	
Comida	Votos
🍎	卌
🍌	|||
🥪	卌 |||

Esta encuesta muestra las comidas favoritas.

T

tally chart A way to show data collected using tally marks. (page 129)

Favorite Foods	
Food	Votes
🍎	卌
🍌	|||
🥪	卌 |||

tabla de conteo Forma de mostrar los datos recogidos utilizando marcas de contar.

Comidas Favoritas	
Comida	Votos
🍎	卌
🍌	|||
🥪	卌 |||

English   **Español**

tens (page 419)

This number has
2 tens.

decenas

Este número tiene
2 decenas.

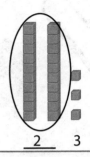

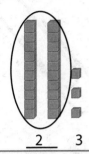

three-dimensional figure
A solid figure. (page 385)

figura de 3 dimensiones
Figura solida.

triangle A shape with three
sides. (page 395)

triángulo Figura con tres
lados.

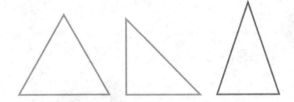

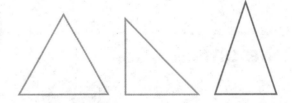

two-dimensional figure
The outline of a figure such
as a triangle, square, or
rectangle. (page 395)

figura de 2 dimensiones
Esquema de una figura
como un triángulo,
cuadrado o rectángulo.

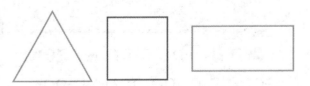

Glossary/Glosario

	English	U	Español

unit An object used to measure. (page 279)

unidad Objeto que se usa para medir.

venn diagram A drawing that uses circles to sort and show data. (page 123)

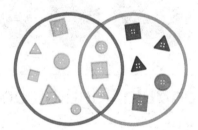

diagrama de Venn Dibujo que utiliza círculos para ordenar y mostrar datos.

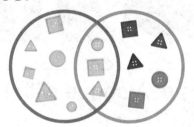

weight (page 285)

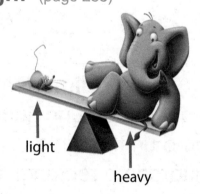

light

heavy

peso

liviano

pesado

zero 0 The number zero equals none or nothing. (page 59)

cero 0 El número cero es igual a nada o ninguno.

Photo Credits

Name _____

Make a Ten (Use with Chapter 9)

1.	4 + 6	6 + 7	5 + 8	8 + 6	4 + 6	8 + 5

2.	2 + 8	5 + 9	9 + 7	1 + 9	3 + 7	7 + 9

3.	7 + 8	5 + 5	6 + 4	7 + 3	9 + 8	4 + 9

- ✂

Name _____

Subtract Zero and All (Use with Chapter 10)

1.	1 − 0	5 − 0	3 − 3	2 − 0	6 − 0	8 − 8

2.	2 − 2	7 − 7	8 − 0	6 − 6	7 − 0	5 − 5

3.	4 − 4	3 − 0	9 − 9	9 − 0	1 − 1	4 − 0

Make a Ten (Use with Chapter 9)

4.
$$
\begin{array}{r} 6 \\ +\,8 \\ \hline \end{array}
\quad
\begin{array}{r} 9 \\ +\,4 \\ \hline \end{array}
\quad
\begin{array}{r} 2 \\ +\,9 \\ \hline \end{array}
\quad
\begin{array}{r} 5 \\ +\,7 \\ \hline \end{array}
\quad
\begin{array}{r} 8 \\ +\,9 \\ \hline \end{array}
\quad
\begin{array}{r} 9 \\ +\,1 \\ \hline \end{array}
$$

5.
$$
\begin{array}{r} 7 \\ +\,7 \\ \hline \end{array}
\quad
\begin{array}{r} 8 \\ +\,2 \\ \hline \end{array}
\quad
\begin{array}{r} 3 \\ +\,8 \\ \hline \end{array}
\quad
\begin{array}{r} 8 \\ +\,4 \\ \hline \end{array}
\quad
\begin{array}{r} 9 \\ +\,6 \\ \hline \end{array}
\quad
\begin{array}{r} 7 \\ +\,3 \\ \hline \end{array}
$$

6.
$$
\begin{array}{r} 9 \\ +\,5 \\ \hline \end{array}
\quad
\begin{array}{r} 6 \\ +\,9 \\ \hline \end{array}
\quad
\begin{array}{r} 4 \\ +\,7 \\ \hline \end{array}
\quad
\begin{array}{r} 7 \\ +\,5 \\ \hline \end{array}
\quad
\begin{array}{r} 8 \\ +\,8 \\ \hline \end{array}
\quad
\begin{array}{r} 3 \\ +\,9 \\ \hline \end{array}
$$

- - - - - - - - - - - - - - - - -

Subtract Zero and All (Use with Chapter 10)

4.
$$
\begin{array}{r} 6 \\ -\,0 \\ \hline \end{array}
\quad
\begin{array}{r} 2 \\ -\,0 \\ \hline \end{array}
\quad
\begin{array}{r} 8 \\ -\,0 \\ \hline \end{array}
\quad
\begin{array}{r} 6 \\ -\,6 \\ \hline \end{array}
\quad
\begin{array}{r} 7 \\ -\,7 \\ \hline \end{array}
\quad
\begin{array}{r} 9 \\ -\,0 \\ \hline \end{array}
$$

5.
$$
\begin{array}{r} 8 \\ -\,8 \\ \hline \end{array}
\quad
\begin{array}{r} 1 \\ -\,1 \\ \hline \end{array}
\quad
\begin{array}{r} 9 \\ -\,9 \\ \hline \end{array}
\quad
\begin{array}{r} 4 \\ -\,0 \\ \hline \end{array}
\quad
\begin{array}{r} 4 \\ -\,4 \\ \hline \end{array}
\quad
\begin{array}{r} 2 \\ -\,2 \\ \hline \end{array}
$$

6.
$$
\begin{array}{r} 3 \\ -\,3 \\ \hline \end{array}
\quad
\begin{array}{r} 5 \\ -\,0 \\ \hline \end{array}
\quad
\begin{array}{r} 7 \\ -\,0 \\ \hline \end{array}
\quad
\begin{array}{r} 1 \\ -\,0 \\ \hline \end{array}
\quad
\begin{array}{r} 3 \\ -\,0 \\ \hline \end{array}
\quad
\begin{array}{r} 5 \\ -\,5 \\ \hline \end{array}
$$

Facts Practice

Name _____

Facts to 10 (Use with Chapter 10)

1. $\begin{array}{r} 4 \\ + 6 \\ \hline \end{array}$ $\begin{array}{r} 4 \\ + 5 \\ \hline \end{array}$ $\begin{array}{r} 3 \\ + 2 \\ \hline \end{array}$ $\begin{array}{r} 2 \\ + 6 \\ \hline \end{array}$ $\begin{array}{r} 2 \\ + 5 \\ \hline \end{array}$ $\begin{array}{r} 1 \\ + 3 \\ \hline \end{array}$

2. $\begin{array}{r} 1 \\ + 7 \\ \hline \end{array}$ $\begin{array}{r} 1 \\ + 1 \\ \hline \end{array}$ $\begin{array}{r} 3 \\ + 7 \\ \hline \end{array}$ $\begin{array}{r} 5 \\ + 1 \\ \hline \end{array}$ $\begin{array}{r} 7 \\ + 3 \\ \hline \end{array}$ $\begin{array}{r} 7 \\ + 2 \\ \hline \end{array}$

3. $\begin{array}{r} 4 \\ + 3 \\ \hline \end{array}$ $\begin{array}{r} 0 \\ + 5 \\ \hline \end{array}$ $\begin{array}{r} 8 \\ + 2 \\ \hline \end{array}$ $\begin{array}{r} 5 \\ + 3 \\ \hline \end{array}$ $\begin{array}{r} 9 \\ + 1 \\ \hline \end{array}$ $\begin{array}{r} 5 \\ + 4 \\ \hline \end{array}$

- ✂

Name _____

Subtract from 10 or Less (Use with Chapter 11)

1. $\begin{array}{r} 10 \\ - 2 \\ \hline \end{array}$ $\begin{array}{r} 9 \\ - 4 \\ \hline \end{array}$ $\begin{array}{r} 10 \\ - 7 \\ \hline \end{array}$ $\begin{array}{r} 10 \\ - 8 \\ \hline \end{array}$ $\begin{array}{r} 9 \\ - 6 \\ \hline \end{array}$ $\begin{array}{r} 10 \\ - 7 \\ \hline \end{array}$

2. $\begin{array}{r} 10 \\ - 4 \\ \hline \end{array}$ $\begin{array}{r} 8 \\ - 6 \\ \hline \end{array}$ $\begin{array}{r} 10 \\ - 1 \\ \hline \end{array}$ $\begin{array}{r} 9 \\ - 7 \\ \hline \end{array}$ $\begin{array}{r} 10 \\ - 9 \\ \hline \end{array}$ $\begin{array}{r} 8 \\ - 5 \\ \hline \end{array}$

3. $\begin{array}{r} 9 \\ - 8 \\ \hline \end{array}$ $\begin{array}{r} 10 \\ - 5 \\ \hline \end{array}$ $\begin{array}{r} 8 \\ - 7 \\ \hline \end{array}$ $\begin{array}{r} 10 \\ - 3 \\ \hline \end{array}$ $\begin{array}{r} 10 \\ - 4 \\ \hline \end{array}$ $\begin{array}{r} 10 \\ - 6 \\ \hline \end{array}$

Facts to 10 (Use with Chapter 10)

4.

5	3	6	9	3	7
+ 5	+ 6	+ 4	+ 1	+ 3	+ 1

5.

1	0	4	5	5	0
+ 6	+ 9	+ 1	+ 3	+ 2	+ 9

6.

3	3	6	7	1	0
+ 4	+ 1	+ 3	+ 0	+ 8	+ 7

- - - - - - - - - - - - - - - - - -

Name _____

Subtract from 10 or Less (Use with Chapter 11)

4.

10	8	10	10	10	10
− 7	− 4	− 9	− 5	− 7	− 3

5.

10	10	10	9	9	10
− 8	− 6	− 4	− 2	− 8	− 8

6.

10	10	10	9	10	9
− 2	− 1	− 6	− 3	− 3	− 6

Facts Practice

Name _____

Facts to 12 (Use with Chapter 11)

1.
$$\begin{array}{r} 3 \\ +5 \\ \hline \end{array}$$
$$\begin{array}{r} 4 \\ +8 \\ \hline \end{array}$$
$$\begin{array}{r} 8 \\ +4 \\ \hline \end{array}$$
$$\begin{array}{r} 0 \\ +8 \\ \hline \end{array}$$
$$\begin{array}{r} 5 \\ +2 \\ \hline \end{array}$$
$$\begin{array}{r} 3 \\ +4 \\ \hline \end{array}$$

2.
$$\begin{array}{r} 6 \\ +5 \\ \hline \end{array}$$
$$\begin{array}{r} 2 \\ +5 \\ \hline \end{array}$$
$$\begin{array}{r} 4 \\ +2 \\ \hline \end{array}$$
$$\begin{array}{r} 9 \\ +1 \\ \hline \end{array}$$
$$\begin{array}{r} 5 \\ +6 \\ \hline \end{array}$$
$$\begin{array}{r} 7 \\ +4 \\ \hline \end{array}$$

3.
$$\begin{array}{r} 5 \\ +4 \\ \hline \end{array}$$
$$\begin{array}{r} 4 \\ +4 \\ \hline \end{array}$$
$$\begin{array}{r} 7 \\ +1 \\ \hline \end{array}$$
$$\begin{array}{r} 0 \\ +6 \\ \hline \end{array}$$
$$\begin{array}{r} 4 \\ +7 \\ \hline \end{array}$$
$$\begin{array}{r} 8 \\ +1 \\ \hline \end{array}$$

- - - - - - - - - - - - - - - - - - - ✂

Name _____

Subtract from 12 or Less (Use with Chapter 12)

1.
$$\begin{array}{r} 12 \\ -9 \\ \hline \end{array}$$
$$\begin{array}{r} 10 \\ -7 \\ \hline \end{array}$$
$$\begin{array}{r} 12 \\ -4 \\ \hline \end{array}$$
$$\begin{array}{r} 12 \\ -7 \\ \hline \end{array}$$
$$\begin{array}{r} 11 \\ -5 \\ \hline \end{array}$$
$$\begin{array}{r} 12 \\ -6 \\ \hline \end{array}$$

2.
$$\begin{array}{r} 12 \\ -3 \\ \hline \end{array}$$
$$\begin{array}{r} 11 \\ -3 \\ \hline \end{array}$$
$$\begin{array}{r} 11 \\ -6 \\ \hline \end{array}$$
$$\begin{array}{r} 11 \\ -2 \\ \hline \end{array}$$
$$\begin{array}{r} 12 \\ -5 \\ \hline \end{array}$$
$$\begin{array}{r} 12 \\ -7 \\ \hline \end{array}$$

3.
$$\begin{array}{r} 12 \\ -6 \\ \hline \end{array}$$
$$\begin{array}{r} 11 \\ -7 \\ \hline \end{array}$$
$$\begin{array}{r} 12 \\ -8 \\ \hline \end{array}$$
$$\begin{array}{r} 11 \\ -8 \\ \hline \end{array}$$
$$\begin{array}{r} 12 \\ -9 \\ \hline \end{array}$$
$$\begin{array}{r} 12 \\ -4 \\ \hline \end{array}$$

Facts to 12 (Use with Chapter 11)

4.
7	4	3	8	2	5
+ 5	+ 3	+ 6	+ 3	+ 4	+ 7

5.
2	2	1	3	6	8
+ 6	+ 2	+ 5	+ 6	+ 6	+ 2

6.
5	6	2	1	9	3
+ 3	+ 4	+ 7	+ 7	+ 2	+ 3

- -

Subtract from 12 or Less (Use with Chapter 12)

4.
12	12	10	12	12	12
− 8	− 9	− 4	− 3	− 4	− 5

5.
12	10	12	10	12	12
− 5	− 8	− 7	− 6	− 8	− 9

6.
11	11	12	12	12	10
− 4	− 9	− 3	− 7	− 6	− 9

Facts Practice

Name _____

Facts to 14 (Use with Chapter 12)

1.
$$\begin{array}{r} 9 \\ + 4 \\ \hline \end{array}\qquad \begin{array}{r} 5 \\ + 3 \\ \hline \end{array}\qquad \begin{array}{r} 7 \\ + 2 \\ \hline \end{array}\qquad \begin{array}{r} 6 \\ + 8 \\ \hline \end{array}\qquad \begin{array}{r} 5 \\ + 8 \\ \hline \end{array}\qquad \begin{array}{r} 4 \\ + 4 \\ \hline \end{array}$$

2.
$$\begin{array}{r} 1 \\ + 6 \\ \hline \end{array}\qquad \begin{array}{r} 0 \\ + 6 \\ \hline \end{array}\qquad \begin{array}{r} 6 \\ + 3 \\ \hline \end{array}\qquad \begin{array}{r} 9 \\ + 0 \\ \hline \end{array}\qquad \begin{array}{r} 7 \\ + 6 \\ \hline \end{array}\qquad \begin{array}{r} 6 \\ + 2 \\ \hline \end{array}$$

3.
$$\begin{array}{r} 7 \\ + 7 \\ \hline \end{array}\qquad \begin{array}{r} 4 \\ + 9 \\ \hline \end{array}\qquad \begin{array}{r} 9 \\ + 5 \\ \hline \end{array}\qquad \begin{array}{r} 1 \\ + 4 \\ \hline \end{array}\qquad \begin{array}{r} 1 \\ + 8 \\ \hline \end{array}\qquad \begin{array}{r} 8 \\ + 5 \\ \hline \end{array}$$

- ✂

Name _____

Subtract from 14 or Less (Use with Chapter 12)

1.
$$\begin{array}{r} 14 \\ - 8 \\ \hline \end{array}\qquad \begin{array}{r} 11 \\ - 5 \\ \hline \end{array}\qquad \begin{array}{r} 14 \\ - 6 \\ \hline \end{array}\qquad \begin{array}{r} 11 \\ - 2 \\ \hline \end{array}\qquad \begin{array}{r} 14 \\ - 9 \\ \hline \end{array}\qquad \begin{array}{r} 14 \\ - 7 \\ \hline \end{array}$$

2.
$$\begin{array}{r} 14 \\ - 5 \\ \hline \end{array}\qquad \begin{array}{r} 13 \\ - 6 \\ \hline \end{array}\qquad \begin{array}{r} 14 \\ - 8 \\ \hline \end{array}\qquad \begin{array}{r} 12 \\ - 8 \\ \hline \end{array}\qquad \begin{array}{r} 12 \\ - 7 \\ \hline \end{array}\qquad \begin{array}{r} 12 \\ - 5 \\ \hline \end{array}$$

3.
$$\begin{array}{r} 13 \\ - 9 \\ \hline \end{array}\qquad \begin{array}{r} 14 \\ - 7 \\ \hline \end{array}\qquad \begin{array}{r} 13 \\ - 8 \\ \hline \end{array}\qquad \begin{array}{r} 14 \\ - 6 \\ \hline \end{array}\qquad \begin{array}{r} 13 \\ - 8 \\ \hline \end{array}\qquad \begin{array}{r} 12 \\ - 9 \\ \hline \end{array}$$

Facts to 14 (Use with Chapter 12)

4.
$$
\begin{array}{r} 6 \\ +4 \\ \hline \end{array}
\qquad
\begin{array}{r} 2 \\ +9 \\ \hline \end{array}
\qquad
\begin{array}{r} 0 \\ +4 \\ \hline \end{array}
\qquad
\begin{array}{r} 5 \\ +9 \\ \hline \end{array}
\qquad
\begin{array}{r} 9 \\ +3 \\ \hline \end{array}
\qquad
\begin{array}{r} 0 \\ +9 \\ \hline \end{array}
$$

5.
$$
\begin{array}{r} 0 \\ +7 \\ \hline \end{array}
\qquad
\begin{array}{r} 3 \\ +8 \\ \hline \end{array}
\qquad
\begin{array}{r} 2 \\ +3 \\ \hline \end{array}
\qquad
\begin{array}{r} 6 \\ +7 \\ \hline \end{array}
\qquad
\begin{array}{r} 3 \\ +7 \\ \hline \end{array}
\qquad
\begin{array}{r} 7 \\ +0 \\ \hline \end{array}
$$

6.
$$
\begin{array}{r} 4 \\ +3 \\ \hline \end{array}
\qquad
\begin{array}{r} 8 \\ +0 \\ \hline \end{array}
\qquad
\begin{array}{r} 3 \\ +2 \\ \hline \end{array}
\qquad
\begin{array}{r} 8 \\ +6 \\ \hline \end{array}
\qquad
\begin{array}{r} 4 \\ +6 \\ \hline \end{array}
\qquad
\begin{array}{r} 5 \\ +1 \\ \hline \end{array}
$$

- -

Subtract from 14 or Less (Use with Chapter 12)

4.
$$
\begin{array}{r} 14 \\ -9 \\ \hline \end{array}
\qquad
\begin{array}{r} 13 \\ -4 \\ \hline \end{array}
\qquad
\begin{array}{r} 14 \\ -8 \\ \hline \end{array}
\qquad
\begin{array}{r} 12 \\ -8 \\ \hline \end{array}
\qquad
\begin{array}{r} 13 \\ -5 \\ \hline \end{array}
\qquad
\begin{array}{r} 14 \\ -5 \\ \hline \end{array}
$$

5.
$$
\begin{array}{r} 11 \\ -5 \\ \hline \end{array}
\qquad
\begin{array}{r} 11 \\ -9 \\ \hline \end{array}
\qquad
\begin{array}{r} 13 \\ -7 \\ \hline \end{array}
\qquad
\begin{array}{r} 14 \\ -6 \\ \hline \end{array}
\qquad
\begin{array}{r} 11 \\ -3 \\ \hline \end{array}
\qquad
\begin{array}{r} 14 \\ -7 \\ \hline \end{array}
$$

6.
$$
\begin{array}{r} 12 \\ -8 \\ \hline \end{array}
\qquad
\begin{array}{r} 14 \\ -7 \\ \hline \end{array}
\qquad
\begin{array}{r} 14 \\ -6 \\ \hline \end{array}
\qquad
\begin{array}{r} 11 \\ -7 \\ \hline \end{array}
\qquad
\begin{array}{r} 14 \\ -9 \\ \hline \end{array}
\qquad
\begin{array}{r} 12 \\ -4 \\ \hline \end{array}
$$

Facts Practice

Name _____

Facts to 16 (Use with Chapter 13)

1.

8	3	5	8	3	2
+ 8	+ 8	+ 2	+ 4	+ 9	+ 5

2.

7	9	8	6	8	9
+ 5	+ 7	+ 6	+ 6	+ 7	+ 6

3.

9	6	5	2	5	7
+ 4	+ 4	+ 8	+ 9	+ 9	+ 8

- - - - - - - - - - - - - - - ✂

Name _____

Subtract from 16 or Less (Use with Chapter 13)

1.

15	13	14	14	15	16
− 9	− 8	− 9	− 6	− 6	− 9

2.

14	16	16	14	13	14
− 7	− 7	− 8	− 8	− 9	− 5

3.

16	15	14	16	16	15
− 9	− 7	− 7	− 7	− 8	− 8

Facts to 16 (Use with Chapter 13)

4.

| $\begin{array}{r}1\\ +8\end{array}$ | $\begin{array}{r}3\\ +8\end{array}$ | $\begin{array}{r}5\\ +7\end{array}$ | $\begin{array}{r}8\\ +5\end{array}$ | $\begin{array}{r}7\\ +4\end{array}$ | $\begin{array}{r}3\\ +5\end{array}$ |

5.

| $\begin{array}{r}7\\ +9\end{array}$ | $\begin{array}{r}7\\ +7\end{array}$ | $\begin{array}{r}7\\ +6\end{array}$ | $\begin{array}{r}6\\ +7\end{array}$ | $\begin{array}{r}5\\ +9\end{array}$ | $\begin{array}{r}9\\ +7\end{array}$ |

6.

| $\begin{array}{r}6\\ +5\end{array}$ | $\begin{array}{r}8\\ +4\end{array}$ | $\begin{array}{r}4\\ +8\end{array}$ | $\begin{array}{r}6\\ +8\end{array}$ | $\begin{array}{r}7\\ +8\end{array}$ | $\begin{array}{r}4\\ +4\end{array}$ |

- - - - - - - - - - - - - - - - - - -

Name _____

Subtract from 16 or Less (Use with Chapter 13)

4.

| $\begin{array}{r}16\\ -9\end{array}$ | $\begin{array}{r}15\\ -9\end{array}$ | $\begin{array}{r}14\\ -7\end{array}$ | $\begin{array}{r}13\\ -5\end{array}$ | $\begin{array}{r}13\\ -7\end{array}$ | $\begin{array}{r}16\\ -9\end{array}$ |

5.

| $\begin{array}{r}15\\ -7\end{array}$ | $\begin{array}{r}12\\ -9\end{array}$ | $\begin{array}{r}13\\ -9\end{array}$ | $\begin{array}{r}16\\ -8\end{array}$ | $\begin{array}{r}13\\ -8\end{array}$ | $\begin{array}{r}13\\ -6\end{array}$ |

6.

| $\begin{array}{r}14\\ -9\end{array}$ | $\begin{array}{r}16\\ -7\end{array}$ | $\begin{array}{r}13\\ -4\end{array}$ | $\begin{array}{r}15\\ -6\end{array}$ | $\begin{array}{r}14\\ -6\end{array}$ | $\begin{array}{r}15\\ -8\end{array}$ |

Facts Practice

Name _____

Facts to 18 (Use with Chapter 15)

1.
$$\begin{array}{r} 8 \\ +9 \\ \hline \end{array}$$
$$\begin{array}{r} 3 \\ +8 \\ \hline \end{array}$$
$$\begin{array}{r} 8 \\ +7 \\ \hline \end{array}$$
$$\begin{array}{r} 9 \\ +8 \\ \hline \end{array}$$
$$\begin{array}{r} 6 \\ +6 \\ \hline \end{array}$$
$$\begin{array}{r} 9 \\ +7 \\ \hline \end{array}$$

2.
$$\begin{array}{r} 0 \\ +8 \\ \hline \end{array}$$
$$\begin{array}{r} 9 \\ +6 \\ \hline \end{array}$$
$$\begin{array}{r} 6 \\ +9 \\ \hline \end{array}$$
$$\begin{array}{r} 6 \\ +3 \\ \hline \end{array}$$
$$\begin{array}{r} 1 \\ +8 \\ \hline \end{array}$$
$$\begin{array}{r} 3 \\ +6 \\ \hline \end{array}$$

3.
$$\begin{array}{r} 3 \\ +9 \\ \hline \end{array}$$
$$\begin{array}{r} 8 \\ +5 \\ \hline \end{array}$$
$$\begin{array}{r} 5 \\ +5 \\ \hline \end{array}$$
$$\begin{array}{r} 2 \\ +7 \\ \hline \end{array}$$
$$\begin{array}{r} 8 \\ +2 \\ \hline \end{array}$$
$$\begin{array}{r} 9 \\ +9 \\ \hline \end{array}$$

- ✂

Name _____

Subtract from 18 or Less (Use with Chapter 14)

1.
$$\begin{array}{r} 18 \\ -9 \\ \hline \end{array}$$
$$\begin{array}{r} 13 \\ -8 \\ \hline \end{array}$$
$$\begin{array}{r} 15 \\ -9 \\ \hline \end{array}$$
$$\begin{array}{r} 14 \\ -5 \\ \hline \end{array}$$
$$\begin{array}{r} 16 \\ -8 \\ \hline \end{array}$$
$$\begin{array}{r} 14 \\ -9 \\ \hline \end{array}$$

2.
$$\begin{array}{r} 16 \\ -7 \\ \hline \end{array}$$
$$\begin{array}{r} 17 \\ -9 \\ \hline \end{array}$$
$$\begin{array}{r} 14 \\ -8 \\ \hline \end{array}$$
$$\begin{array}{r} 16 \\ -9 \\ \hline \end{array}$$
$$\begin{array}{r} 13 \\ -9 \\ \hline \end{array}$$
$$\begin{array}{r} 18 \\ -9 \\ \hline \end{array}$$

3.
$$\begin{array}{r} 17 \\ -8 \\ \hline \end{array}$$
$$\begin{array}{r} 14 \\ -7 \\ \hline \end{array}$$
$$\begin{array}{r} 14 \\ -6 \\ \hline \end{array}$$
$$\begin{array}{r} 15 \\ -6 \\ \hline \end{array}$$
$$\begin{array}{r} 15 \\ -8 \\ \hline \end{array}$$
$$\begin{array}{r} 13 \\ -7 \\ \hline \end{array}$$

Name _____

Facts to 18 (Use with Chapter 15)

4.
$$\begin{array}{r} 9 \\ +\ 8 \\ \hline \end{array} \qquad \begin{array}{r} 1 \\ +\ 6 \\ \hline \end{array} \qquad \begin{array}{r} 2 \\ +\ 9 \\ \hline \end{array} \qquad \begin{array}{r} 4 \\ +\ 9 \\ \hline \end{array} \qquad \begin{array}{r} 7 \\ +\ 6 \\ \hline \end{array} \qquad \begin{array}{r} 4 \\ +\ 2 \\ \hline \end{array}$$

5.
$$\begin{array}{r} 3 \\ +\ 4 \\ \hline \end{array} \qquad \begin{array}{r} 8 \\ +\ 4 \\ \hline \end{array} \qquad \begin{array}{r} 8 \\ +\ 9 \\ \hline \end{array} \qquad \begin{array}{r} 4 \\ +\ 5 \\ \hline \end{array} \qquad \begin{array}{r} 6 \\ +\ 4 \\ \hline \end{array} \qquad \begin{array}{r} 5 \\ +\ 8 \\ \hline \end{array}$$

6.
$$\begin{array}{r} 9 \\ +\ 2 \\ \hline \end{array} \qquad \begin{array}{r} 9 \\ +\ 9 \\ \hline \end{array} \qquad \begin{array}{r} 5 \\ +\ 7 \\ \hline \end{array} \qquad \begin{array}{r} 6 \\ +\ 8 \\ \hline \end{array} \qquad \begin{array}{r} 7 \\ +\ 9 \\ \hline \end{array} \qquad \begin{array}{r} 5 \\ +\ 9 \\ \hline \end{array}$$

- - - - - - - - - - - - - - - - - - - -

Name _____

Subtract from 18 or Less (Use with Chapter 15)

4.
$$\begin{array}{r} 13 \\ -\ 6 \\ \hline \end{array} \qquad \begin{array}{r} 12 \\ -\ 4 \\ \hline \end{array} \qquad \begin{array}{r} 12 \\ -\ 9 \\ \hline \end{array} \qquad \begin{array}{r} 18 \\ -\ 9 \\ \hline \end{array} \qquad \begin{array}{r} 13 \\ -\ 4 \\ \hline \end{array} \qquad \begin{array}{r} 12 \\ -\ 7 \\ \hline \end{array}$$

5.
$$\begin{array}{r} 13 \\ -\ 5 \\ \hline \end{array} \qquad \begin{array}{r} 16 \\ -\ 9 \\ \hline \end{array} \qquad \begin{array}{r} 16 \\ -\ 8 \\ \hline \end{array} \qquad \begin{array}{r} 15 \\ -\ 8 \\ \hline \end{array} \qquad \begin{array}{r} 16 \\ -\ 7 \\ \hline \end{array} \qquad \begin{array}{r} 17 \\ -\ 8 \\ \hline \end{array}$$

6.
$$\begin{array}{r} 12 \\ -\ 8 \\ \hline \end{array} \qquad \begin{array}{r} 12 \\ -\ 5 \\ \hline \end{array} \qquad \begin{array}{r} 18 \\ -\ 9 \\ \hline \end{array} \qquad \begin{array}{r} 17 \\ -\ 9 \\ \hline \end{array} \qquad \begin{array}{r} 15 \\ -\ 9 \\ \hline \end{array} \qquad \begin{array}{r} 12 \\ -\ 6 \\ \hline \end{array}$$

WorkMat 1

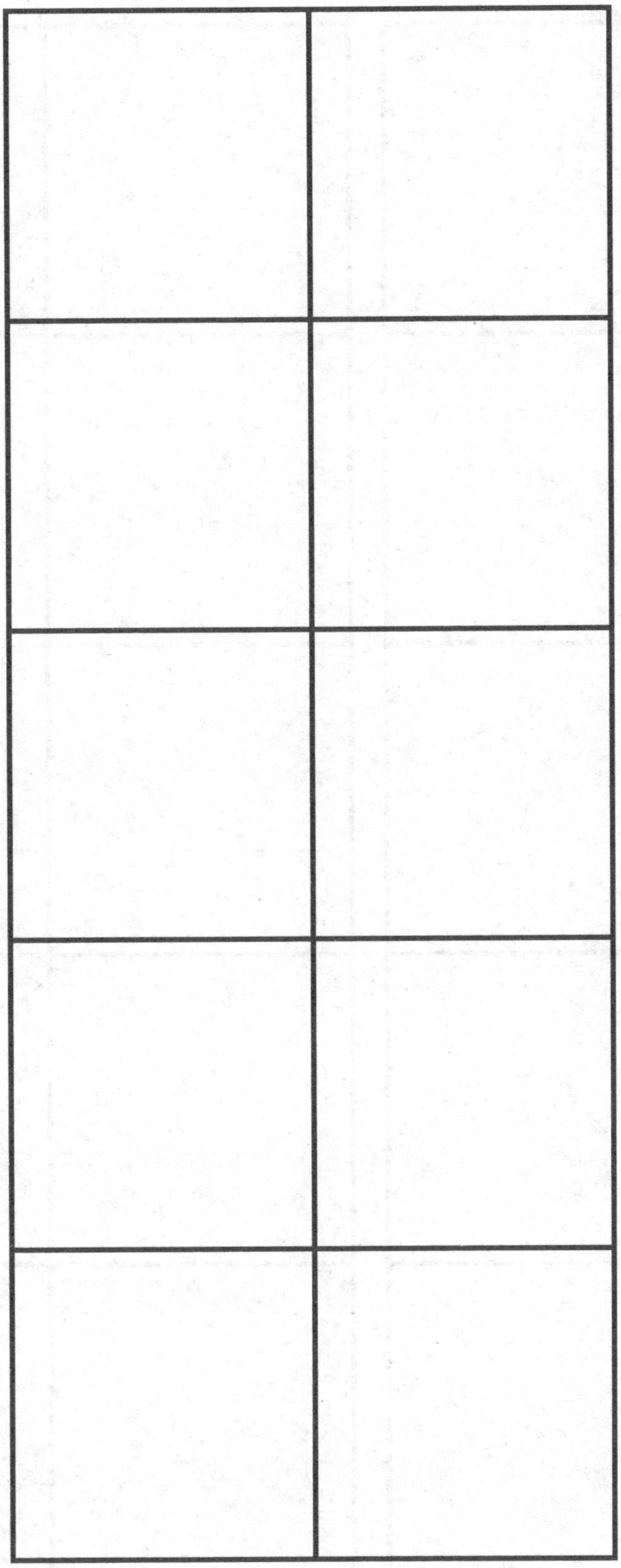

WorkMat 1: Ten-Frame

WorkMat 2: Ten-Frames

WorkMat 3

Part	Part

Whole

WorkMat 3: Part-Part-Whole

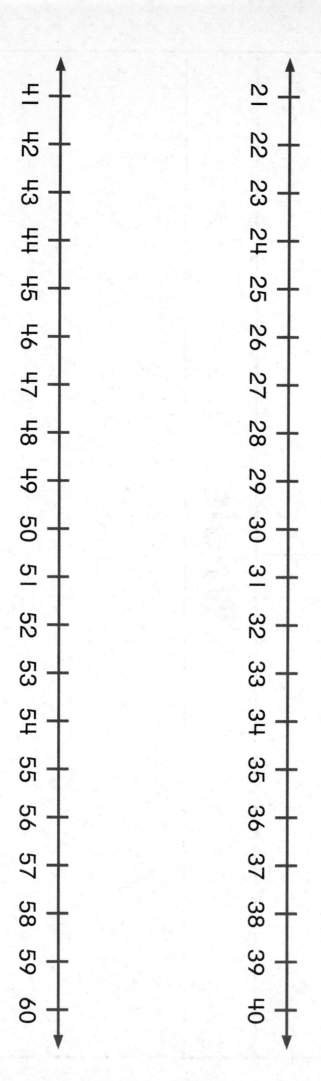

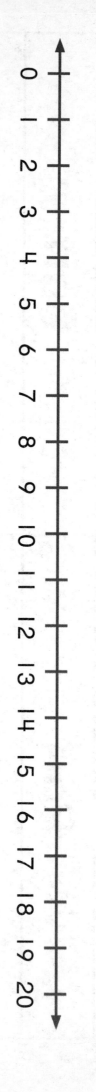

WorkMat 4: Number Lines

WorkMat 5

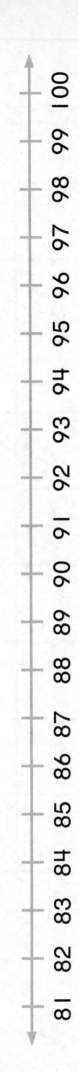

WorkMat 5: Number Lines

WorkMat 6: Grid

Tens	Ones

WorkMat 7: Tens and Ones Chart

Hundreds	Tens	Ones

WorkMat 8: Hundreds, Tens, and Ones Chart